OMG Pancakes!

OMG Pancakes!

75 COOL CREATIONS Your KIDS Will Love to EAT

JIM BELOSIC

AVERY • A MEMBER OF PENGUIN GROUP (USA) INC. • NEW YORK

Published by the Penguin Group
Penguin Group (USA) Inc., 375 Hudson Street, New York, New York 10014, USA • Penguin Group (Canada),
90 Eglinton Avenue East, Suite 700, Toronto, Ontario M4P 2Y3, Canada (a division of Pearson Penguin Canada Inc.) •
Penguin Books Ltd, 80 Strand, London WC2R 0RL, England • Penguin Ireland, 25 St Stephen's Green, Dublin 2,
Ireland (a division of Penguin Books Ltd) • Penguin Group (Australia), 250 Camberwell Road,
Camberwell, Victoria 3124, Australia (a division of Pearson Australia Group Pty Ltd) • Penguin Books India Pvt Ltd,
11 Community Centre, Panchsheel Park, New Delhi–110 017, India • Penguin Group (NZ), 67 Apollo Drive,
Rosedale, North Shore 0632, New Zealand (a division of Pearson New Zealand Ltd) • Penguin Books
(South Africa) (Pty) Ltd, 24 Sturdee Avenue, Rosebank, Johannesburg 2196, South Africa

Penguin Books Ltd, Registered Offices: 80 Strand, London WC2R 0RL, England

Most Avery books are available at special quantity discounts for bulk purchase for sales promotions, premiums,
fund-raising, and educational needs. Special books or book excerpts also can be created to fit specific needs.
For details, write Penguin Group (USA) Inc. Special Markets, 375 Hudson Street, New York, NY 10014.

Library of Congress Cataloging-in-Publication Data

Belosic, Jim.
OMG pancakes! : 75 cool creations your kids will love to eat / Jim Belosic.
p.   cm.
ISBN 978-1-58333-443-0
1. Pancakes, waffles, etc.   2. Cookbooks.   I. Title.
TX770.P34B45   2011   2011026889
641.81'53—dc23

Printed in the United States of America
1   3   5   7   9   10   8   6   4   2

BOOK DESIGN BY MEIGHAN CAVANAUGH

ILLUSTRATIONS BY LEA HECKLEY

PHOTOGRAPHS BY CANDICE NYANDO

The recipes contained in this book are to be followed exactly as written. The publisher is not
responsible for specific health or allergy needs that may require medical supervision. The
publisher is not responsible for any adverse reactions to the recipes contained in this book.

While the author has made every effort to provide accurate telephone numbers and Internet addresses
at the time of publication, neither the publisher nor the author assumes any responsibility for errors,
or for changes that occur after publication. Further, the publisher does not have any control over
and does not assume any responsibility for author or third-party websites or their content.

To Allie and Ryan.

Thank you for helping to make our

breakfast time so much fun. I know that I'll

always remember making pancakes for you guys;

I hope you remember these times too.

Love, Dad

CONTENTS

OMG Pancakes!

1

INTRODUCTION

My dad probably made me breakfast two times in my entire life. Like most dads, Martha Stewart he was not. But here's the thing—the times he made me breakfast are the only times I can really remember anyone making me breakfast. Each time he made pancakes—generally a foolproof endeavor—and of course he messed them up. He honestly didn't know what the heck he was doing. He tried to make Mickey Mouse and it came out all lopsided, as if it were Mickey Mouse interpreted by Dalí. He put it in front of me and said in his gruff voice, "It's the moon," and then, "Look! A cucumber!" and then, "Just eat the darn thing."

I don't know whether it was the simple fact that he took the time to make me breakfast, or that his creations were amazing to my young imagination, even if they fell well short of his own grand visions (or maybe that's what he envisioned). To me, my dad's pancakes made him the coolest guy ever. He took something so ordinary—pancakes for breakfast—and turned it into something more exciting than it had any right to be.

So last year, when I put a poodle-shaped pancake in front of my three-year-old daughter, Allie, it was a hit. In truth, it looked very little like a poodle (there goes the Dalí interpretation again), but she dug it, which was the whole point. The memories of my dad's breakfasts came back to me, and I realized I'd hit upon something she and I could share together. The requests quickly started rolling in for princesses, castles, elephants . . . and before I knew it, we had a little Saturday-morning ritual. My wife would go to Starbucks and have a little quiet time while Allie and I made pancakes together. She mixed the batter and decided what shape we'd go for that day, and I'd do whatever I could to make it happen.

The pancakes rapidly started getting complex, going from little animal shapes to full-blown structures. The first big one was a construction crane, which I pieced together by making four flat lattice pieces that I "glued" together with pancake batter and a lighter—a process that, as I'll explain later in this book, isn't for the faint of heart. But the thing worked, unbelievably.

I'll admit that, on occasion, Allie loses interest long before I do. My hardest project to date, a Ferris wheel, took hours to finish and resulted in several burned fingers. When I finally finished it, Allie, whose belly was already full of pancakes, was too absorbed in television to care. I proudly showed my wife, whose response was, "Hey, that's cool. Does it spin?"

"No," I said, sheepishly.

"Hmph," she said, and walked away. I ate that one alone.

I never had illusions that this project would become anything more than a fun father-daughter tradition. But I don't mind saying I was kind of proud of our creations, so I would usually snap a quick photo of them with my phone and put them on my blog so my family and friends could see them. One day, a strange error message popped up on my website that indicated my server was down. Apparently there had been a big traffic spike, which made no sense to me. I wrote it off as a glitch, but it kept happening. I started doing a little research, and the analytics showed that my little website had found a big audience.

My first thought was, Who the heck are all these people checking out my pancake pictures? I couldn't imagine how they found me, but further research told me my site had been picked up by AOL, YouTube, and a few other major sites.

Pretty soon, strangers were writing to me, saying things like: "I saw what you did, I tried it with my kids this weekend, and it was so much fun. Thanks for the inspiration!" My site was getting mentions in *Esquire* and *Redbook* magazines, and I was asked to appear on a few morning shows. I even spent two hours taking pancake requests from the audience at *Good Day Sacramento*. And my Facebook page, Jim's Pancakes, now has something like 29,000 fans.

Meanwhile, my system has gotten a little more refined. I've come up with a few natural alternatives to food coloring, which has opened up quite a few color options, and I now use several restaurant-quality squeeze bottles to apply batter very precisely to the griddle.

Sophisticated, I know.

I don't claim to be any kind of chef, but I've figured out a few tricks I can share with you if you decide to give this a try. The designs have ranged from animals to fake food (spaghetti in a bowl, bacon and eggs, that kind of thing) to natural and man-made phenomena (a volcano, a bridge).

The little boy inside me is dying to make some *Star Wars* pancakes—the *Millennium Falcon*, the Death Star. Someday soon, when my twelve-month-old son is old enough to appreciate it, we'll give those a try. But right now, it's all still about Allie. She's four, and her requests continue to tend toward the girly . . . princesses, unicorns, and such. I'm still cranking away on new designs, but it's still really just about that Saturday-morning ritual, just for the two of us. She pulls up a chair to stand on and watches anxiously as I heat up the griddle and throw on that test pancake, which she always gets to eat. And so begins a pancake-eating extravaganza that lasts an hour or two, until she gets full.

As strange as it's been to get so much attention for the breakfasts I make for my daughter, it's also pretty gratifying. It's made me realize that maybe people are so interested in this ambitious little pancake project because, at the heart of it, we're all just looking for ways to get our kids to think we're cool. At least I hope Allie thinks I am.

And who doesn't love pancakes?

TOOLS OF
THE TRADE

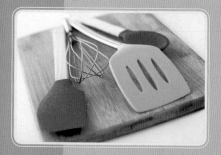

These are the key tools that I've found are best for making the creations in this book, though you can certainly use other tools you have lying around your house as well.

- **Nonstick griddle (electric or stovetop, preferably cast-iron)**
Using a nonstick griddle helps retain the color of the batter. If you use butter or oil to coat the pan, it could make your pancake become discolored. I prefer cast-iron because it heats evenly and maintains temperature very well. Avoid thin skillets, because with them you'll get hot spots that could burn your creations.

- **Squeeze bottles**
Plastic squeeze bottles are the key ingredient for pancake art. They allow you to draw with the batter just like a crayon. I typically get bottles from a local restaurant supply store; sometimes you can even find them in the grocery store or order them online (you can get them for a couple bucks). If you're in a pinch, old ketchup bottles work great, too!

- **Plastic bags**
An alternative to squeeze bottles or used ketchup bottles. They are also great because there's no cleanup involved after you're done. Fill them up with some batter and cut a small piece off one corner—instant pancake pen.

A good pancake flipper

Unless you have some insanely high threshold for pain or you're possibly one of the X-Men, you'll need one of these to flip some of the pancakes you're cooking. I usually try to find the biggest one I can get so that it's easier to flip the big pieces (check out www.jimspancakes.com/store for a few of my favorites). If you're working on a nonstick Teflon griddle, use a plastic model so that you don't scratch the surface.

Whisk

For getting the clumps out of your batter, this is a must.

A good spatula

This tool is useful for scraping as much batter as you can out of your bowls.

Funnel

This one makes it easier to get your batter into bottles than pouring it manually from the bowl. Unless you have incredible skill for pinpoint accuracy!

Cooking torch or lighter

What you need to help set your projects in 3-D.

Damp towel

This is for cleaning your griddle. Always maintain your tools! This also keeps your partner happy with the perception of your tidiness.

Patience and persistence

For some of these creations, you'll need a wellspring of patience and persistence. Honestly, this is just useful advice for life.

PANCAKE RECIPES AND FOOD COLORING INGREDIENTS

Standard Pancake Recipe

Here is the standard pancake recipe I use. It usually produces 8 to 12 pancakes about 4 inches (10 centimeters) in diameter. Feel free to adjust the recipe for quantity or quality, depending on what you'd like. I usually make 2 or 3 batches to use for a pancake project, and if I have leftovers, I usually cook them up or store them in the fridge for the next day. Make sure you mix the batter well before creating your portions.

The following directions are for a standard round pancake, so if you want to make plain-old "moon" pancakes, then you can still use this recipe. My father would be proud of you.

1 cup all-purpose flour
2 teaspoons baking powder
2 tablespoons sugar
1/4 teaspoon salt
1 large egg
1 cup milk
2 tablespoons melted butter

Preheat the griddle.

In medium bowl, stir or sift the flour, baking powder, sugar, and salt together. In another bowl, beat the egg, milk, and butter together. Stir your wet mixture into the dry ingredients until the batter is extremely smooth. Remember, you're working from squeeze bottles, ketchup bottles, or even plastic bags to draw specific lines with your pancake batter. Any lumps will just keep you from getting a smooth delivery!

For pancake art, slowly squeeze the batter onto a nonstick hot griddle (300 to 325 degrees). Flip the pancake when bubbles appear on the surface (after about 2 to 3 minutes), or sooner if you are trying to keep the colors light. You need to turn these pancakes only once.

Here are some variations for more healthful alternatives. **Keep in mind that they may change the color and consistency of the batter.** If you're really intent on sticking with a theme, like the banana pancakes for the Monkey—or even the Banana!—just swap out either the dry or the wet ingredients as needed.

Whole Wheat Pancakes

Substitute whole wheat flour for the all-purpose flour and brown sugar for the regular sugar. Again, be cautious, as this changes the consistency and final color of your pancake. If you add color to whole wheat pancakes, stick with darker colors, since the lighter colors may not come out as bright.

Pumpkin Pancakes

Add 2/3 cup pumpkin puree, 1/2 teaspoon ground cinnamon, and 1/4 teaspoon ground ginger to the batter before you do the final mixing. This could spice things up for Halloween!

Banana Pancakes

Add a well-mashed banana to the batter before you do the final mixing. Remember, good runny batter—even with a mashed banana—is the key!

Apple Pancakes

Add 3/4 cup applesauce to the batter with the wet ingredients.

Buttermilk Pancakes

Substitute buttermilk for the regular milk and add 1/4 teaspoon baking soda to the dry ingredients.

Blueberry Pancakes

Add fresh or frozen blueberries to the batter after you've blended out all the lumps. You may not be able to squeeze the blueberries out of your squeeze bottle, though, and may want to use the plastic-baggie technique instead. Berries are great for making a spotted animal.

Orange-Flavored Pancakes

Add 1/2 teaspoon orange zest to the batter before the final mix.

Bacon Pancakes

Add 1/4 cup finely crumbled bacon to the batter after the final mix. The batter may be hard to squeeze through a squeeze bottle, so you may want to try the plastic-baggie approach instead. If you're looking at the Bacon 'n' Eggs (page 101), then you definitely want to try this one, especially if you miss having actual bacon with your meal. I know I do!

Note: If you don't have the time to make pancakes from scratch, a store-bought mix will do the trick. Krusteaz Buttermilk Pancakes is the brand of choice in our house. Just be sure to mix the batter well so that there are no lumps that could clog up your squeeze bottles and ruin your pancake creations.

NATURAL FOOD COLORING

Putting any sort of food coloring into something you're about to eat may set off some red flags. That's why I try to make my own natural food coloring whenever possible. It's more fun, too! When using these food colorings, make sure to blend them well with the batter so that the batter is still smooth and easy to work with. When you're using juice or any other natural coloring, make sure to use enough to color the batter but not so much that it overpowers the pancakes with its taste. I usually start with a small amount and add a little at a time until I get the desired color. Here are a few options for natural food coloring:

- Natural red—seedless strawberry jam, raspberry jam, beet juice
- Natural orange—orange juice concentrate, canned pumpkin, carrot juice, orange-colored jam (apricot, peach)
- Natural brown—cocoa powder, melted chocolate chips, chocolate syrup
- Natural green—avocado (make sure to mash the fruit thoroughly and to use just enough to achieve a green color)
- Natural blue—blueberries (fresh or frozen; a few make a nice lavender color; a lot make blue), blueberry jam

Some colors are tough to achieve without using some food coloring. Bright green, yellow, and blue are hard to create without some kind of dye. You can buy natural food coloring at health food stores and Whole Foods; just add a few drops to the batter. Again, be careful with portions or you will wind up with some garish neon batter—although with enough green you could make a cool Slimer pancake!

TIPS
AND
TRICKS

Whe you're making your pancake creations, always keep the following tips and tricks in mind. As the saying goes, "Work smarter, not harder."

Guidelines for preparation:

1. If you're in a hurry or don't want to make a huge mess, skip the standard pancake recipe and use a store-bought mix. Krusteaz works great—just mix it up longer than they recommend on the box.

2. Make sure you mix the batter well. Clumps will clog up the squeeze bottle. I use a handheld immersion mixer to blend the batter. Allie loves to use the mixer, but it can turn to chaos very quickly.

3. Add water to the batter until the mixture can flow from the squeeze bottle well. It should be about the consistency of thick mustard.

4. Mix one big batch of batter and then split it into small bowls to add individual coloring. Adding coloring is another opportunity to involve the kids.

5. Use a French coffee press or a fine-meshed sieve to strain out juice for coloring ingredients such as raspberries.

6. When adding juice coloring to the batter, such as beet juice for red or orange juice concentrate for orange, add the juice in place of the water so it doesn't get too runny. You can always add more water at the end.

7. When using food coloring, don't use too much, as it will make the food look really weird. Bright blue pancakes are scary. Sky blue seems more edible.

8. Never try to make black pancake batter. It comes out gray and gross. I've tried, trust me. Try cocoa powder instead and go for dark brown.

9. Refrigerate any leftover batter and use it the next day—one day is about the maximum storage time.

Drawing with squeeze bottles:

1. Plan out your design in your head or try it on paper first.
2. Start with your outline first, applying steady pressure to the bottle.
3. After your outline is done, fill in the middle in a quick, smooth motion.
4. To make it easier, create your design in multiple pieces so you will be drawing only simple shapes.
5. Follow my instructive illustrations for each project to construct the pieces together.

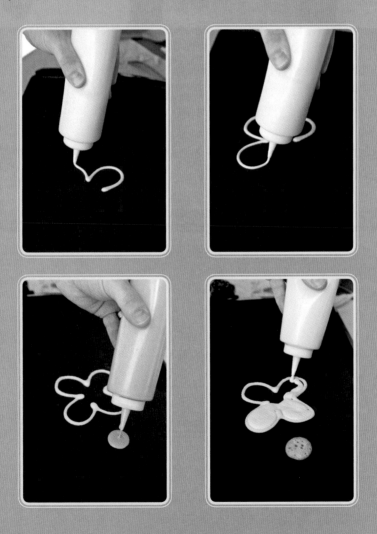

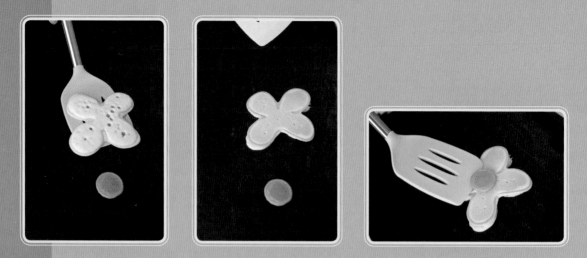

For the squeeze bottles, utensils, and the griddle itself:

1. Buy squeeze bottles at a restaurant supply store; they cost only a couple of bucks.
2. No squeeze bottles? Try an old ketchup bottle. Don't have one? Cut the corner off of a sandwich bag. Plastic bags work great and the cleanup is easy.
3. Use a nonstick griddle. Using butter or oil when you're cooking will cause your pancakes to get discolored. Unless you're going for that look!
4. Use *only* plastic pancake flippers on nonstick surfaces. I'm sure you know this, but in case you don't, just trust me.

Guidelines for cooking:

1. Keep the griddle at 300 to 325 degrees, no higher, to prevent discoloring and burning the pancakes. The goal is to cook slowly so that you have time to draw the outlines or shapes you need.
2. If you need to flip the pancake early to preserve color, that's fine. You can cook it more on the other side.
3. Work fast—you have only a couple of minutes before the pancakes start to burn!
4. If you're making 3-D shapes, cook the pancakes longer so they can stand up well. They still taste good; they'll just be crispy on the outside.

If you're married:

1. Clean up afterward—otherwise your spouse will not appreciate pancake day after a couple of weekends. Again, trust me on this!

5

ANIMALS, REAL AND IMAGINED

Alligator

· ·

You're going to want to eat this pancake before he eats you. Much tastier than the real thing.

PREPARATION

For this recipe, you will need:

- Plain pancake batter
- Natural green food coloring
- Two squeeze bottles (or plastic bags; see page 8)
- Chocolate chips

Split the batter into two parts in two separate bowls, with the larger portion about three-fourths of the batter. Add green food coloring to the larger portion and leave the smaller portion plain. Transfer the batter into two separate squeeze bottles.

CREATE

Let's start with the green batter and make an outline for the shape of the alligator. Fill him in and add some ridges to his back.

On the side of the griddle, make a couple of green legs.

Then, with your plain batter, make two small circles. This is what you will use for the eyes. Make some teeth with the plain batter and attach them to the alligator's mouth. An alligator isn't an alligator without his teeth!

Flip the alligator. Once he is nice and cooked, carefully remove all his pieces from the heat. (It could be a she as well; I'll leave that up to you.)

PLATE

Place the body flat on the plate. Now add the legs and the circles for the eyes. The finishing touch is the chocolate chips for the eyeballs. See ya later, alligator!

Lion's Head

It's time to take "pride" in your pancake creations and tame the King of the Jungle! He's also quite delicious.

PREPARATION

For this recipe, you will need:

- Plain pancake batter
- Natural brown food coloring
- Natural yellow food coloring
- Natural red food coloring
- Four squeeze bottles (or plastic bags; see page 8)
- Chocolate chips

Split the batter into four parts in four separate bowls, with two portions each about twice as large as each of the two others. Add brown food coloring to one of the larger portions and yellow to the other. Add red food coloring to one of the smaller portions and leave the other small portion plain. Transfer the batter into four separate squeeze bottles.

CREATE

Using the brown batter, start cooking the lion's mane. Just imagine creating the mane in the outline of the sun or a circular saw. Fill in the rest of the mane with the brown batter. After letting the mane brown (no pun intended) on both sides, move it to the plate.

Then make the face with the yellow batter by cooking a regular round pancake.

When you have finished the face, remove it from the griddle and start working on the ears. Keeping with the yellow batter, create two small triangle outlines. Then use your red batter to put a small dot inside each triangle. Let the outline and the red dots cook for a little, then fill in the rest of the triangles with the yellow batter.

With the red batter, lay down a smaller triangle on the griddle and cook on both sides. This will be the lion's nose. Set aside.

To create the mouth, with the brown batter, make the shape of an anchor or an upturned wishbone. You could also make it in the shape of a downturned wishbone to give your lion a frown, which actually could work, since you're going to eat him!

Create two small pancakes with the plain batter for the eyes. Let them cook on both sides. Now you're ready for plating.

PLATE

Set the mane down on the plate first. Next, lay down the yellow pancake and the ears to form the face. Place the two plain-batter pancakes for the eyes where appropriate in the larger yellow pancake and the red-triangle nose just below them near the center. Set the mouth below the nose. Take two chocolate chips and set one on each eye, and there you have it. This is definitely a dish to roar about!

Ladybug

· ·

Who doesn't like ladybugs? Especially ladybugs that taste as good as this one!

PREPARATION

For this recipe, you will need:

- Plain pancake batter
- Natural brown food coloring
- Natural red food coloring
- Two squeeze bottles (or plastic bags; see page 8)

Split the batter into two equal parts in two separate bowls. Add red food coloring to one part and brown to the other. Transfer the batter into two separate squeeze bottles.

CREATE

Grab your brown batter. Make two circles, one about twice the size of the other, for the body and head. Attach antennae to the head.

Next, get your red batter and get ready for action. Make two half-circles for the wings. Fill them in with the red batter, leaving several small circles open for the spots. Fill in those small circles with brown batter.

When the ladybug parts have cooked through on both sides, remove them from the heat.

PLATE

Place the body on the plate first. Now you can layer on the wings, as shown in the illustration. It's cute as a bug!

Cute Little Caterpillar

This little green caterpillar is more cute than creepy!

PREPARATION

For this recipe, you will need:

- Plain pancake batter
- Natural green food coloring
- Natural yellow food coloring
- One squeeze bottle (or plastic bag; see page 8)
- Chocolate chips

Split the batter into two parts in two separate bowls, with one portion the majority of the total and the other just a tiny amount. Add green food coloring to the larger portion, and yellow to the other. Transfer the green batter to a squeeze bottle, and set the yellow portion aside.

CREATE

Make all the legs first—you can decide how many. The trick is to make them pretty short so they can hold the weight of the caterpillar's body. Using the green batter, make outlines and then fill them in. Cook, letting them get a little crisp on one side for strength.

Now start on the body. The body is just a progression of circles (again, you decide how many), perhaps getting a little smaller at the end. You don't flip the body for this one. Just let it cook all the way through on one side on a low griddle temperature. Right before the batter is cooked completely, stick the legs on and they'll cook with the body.

On the side of the griddle, use the green to make the caterpillar's head with antennae. Take the yellow batter and add some color to the tip of the antennae.

Once all the parts are cooked, remove them from the heat.

PLATE

Put your skills to the test and remove your caterpillar from the griddle, without breaking him into pieces, so he stands on his legs. Attach the head with batter as "glue": apply a touch of either color batter and "cook" it with a lighter until the head is on securely. Give him some eyes with two chocolate chips. This caterpillar won't give you butterflies!

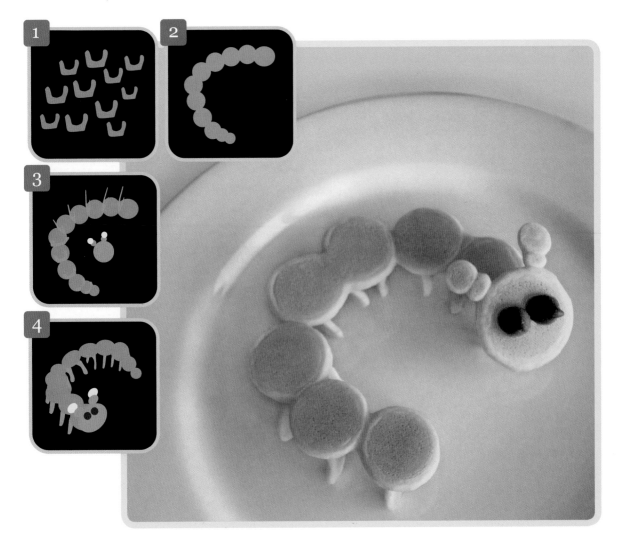

Bees and Beehive

. . . .

Bees for your busy bees. This is a breakfast to buzz about.

PREPARATION

For this recipe, you will need:

- Plain pancake batter
- Natural brown food coloring
- Natural yellow food coloring
- Three squeeze bottles (or plastic bags; see page 8)

Split the batter into three parts in three separate bowls. One part should be twice as large as each of the other two; this largest portion is to remain plain. Add brown food coloring and yellow food coloring separately to each of the other two portions. Transfer the batter into three separate squeeze bottles.

CREATE

Start with the hive. This is pretty easy: With plain batter, make one large filled-in circle for the bottom, then make pieces to stack by reducing the size of each subsequent circle. The bottom part of the beehive is made from larger open circles; the top part is small full circles. Once the circles are cooked, set them aside.

Next, let's make some bees for that hive. Draw the heads and tails with the brown batter. Fill in the bodies and wings with the yellow batter. You can make as many bees as you see fit.

When the bees have been flipped once and are finished cooking on both sides, remove them from the heat.

PLATE

Starting with the largest circle, stack the pieces of the hive. Add some bees to the plate and serve. Try honey instead of syrup for a sweet and healthy topping. These pancakes are the bee's knees!

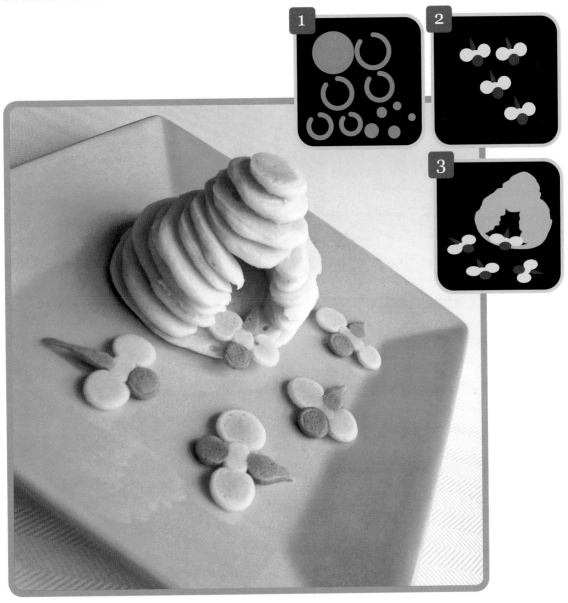

Crab

· ·

Feeling crabby? This pancake should cheer you right up!

PREPARATION

For this recipe, you will need:

- Plain pancake batter
- Natural red food coloring
- One squeeze bottle (or plastic bag; see page 8)
- Chocolate chips

Divide your batter into two parts in two separate bowls. One part will be the majority of the batter and the other will be just a tiny amount for the eyes. Add red food coloring to the larger portion and leave the other batter plain. Transfer the red batter to a squeeze bottle, and set the plain portion aside.

CREATE

First, using the red batter, make the shapes of the crab, starting with an outline and filling it in. The body is a basic oval shape. When you make the legs, let the outline cook for a bit so that there is a distinction between the oval shape of the body and the legs. Keep the legs connected to the body.

Next, make the pincers for the crab, again using the red batter and starting with an outline and filling it in. The pincers are each their own shape and will be added on top of the body section when you do the plating. Make sure you remember to make them facing opposite directions!

On the side of the griddle, using your plain batter, make two small circles for the eyes.

When the circles have cooked on both sides, remove them from the heat.

PLATE

Now for the assembly. Start by placing the body and legs on the plate; the pincers come next. Finally, place chocolate chips on the two eye circles. Ta-da. You have a crab!

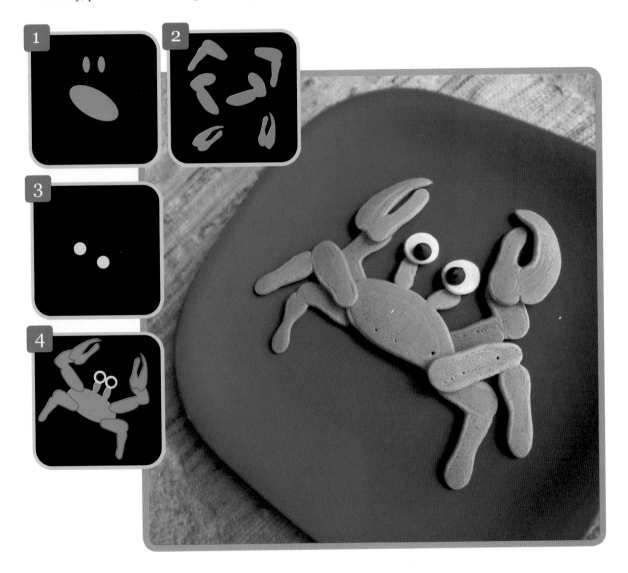

Elephant

· ·

How do you fit an elephant onto a plate? Make it a pancake!

PREPARATION

For this recipe, you will need:

- Plain pancake batter
- One squeeze bottle (or plastic bag; see page 8)
- Chocolate chips

Put your plain pancake batter into a squeeze bottle.

CREATE

This one is pretty simple, as it's just a bunch of shapes. You'll make an outline for each shape and then fill it in. Let's start with the body and head by making two large circles, one a bit larger than the other. On the side, make the ears, trunk, legs, eyes, and tail. Fill all of the pieces in.

Once the pieces are cooked on both sides, remove them from the heat.

PLATE

Let's start by layering the elephant. Lay down the tail first, then the body, then the head. Next, the legs, the eyes, the ears, and the trunk. Place two chocolate chips on the eyes, and your elephant is ready to eat. You'd better make some room in your belly!

Puppy Dog

. . . .

How much is that puppy on my plate? Only the time it takes to make him, and he won't chew your shoes.

PREPARATION

For this recipe, you will need:

- Plain pancake batter
- Natural brown food coloring
- Natural red food coloring
- Two squeeze bottles (or plastic bags; see page 8)
- Chocolate chips

Split the batter into three parts in three separate bowls. Take one very small amount out for the tongue; then divide the rest into two equal portions. Add brown food coloring to one of the larger portions and leave the other large portion plain. Add red food coloring to the smallest portion. Transfer the brown batter and plain batter into two separate squeeze bottles. The small red portion can be left aside.

CREATE

The puppy is basically made up of a lot of circles, just different sizes. With your plain batter, start making the outlines of all the different circles and ovals. You will need a body, a head, three legs, one of the ears, and a tail. Oh, and don't forget to make small circles for the whites of his eyes. Fill these all in. If you look at the illustration, you will see that I left some open areas here for the brown.

Once the plain areas are all filled in, grab your brown batter. Start filling in the areas you left open for the nose, mouth, and some spots. Off to the side of the griddle, make the other ear with the brown batter.

That griddle is hot and your puppy is going to need his tongue. With your red batter, make a little tongue off to the side.

Cook all pieces thoroughly and remove them from the heat.

PLATE

We're going to add the pieces in layers. Start with the two ears and the tail. Next add the body, then the head and legs. Last, add the whites of his eyes, two chocolate chips for the eyeballs, and his tongue. This puppy is ready for the table!

Octopus

· ·

Widen your pancake palate with seafood for breakfast. This octopus is a fun and easy way to liven up your morning. Or evening. There's nothing wrong with pancakes for dinner.

PREPARATION

For this recipe, you will need:

- Plain pancake batter
- Natural green food coloring—or any color, really
- One squeeze bottle (or plastic bag; see page 8)
- Chocolate chips

Color the pancake batter with food coloring. Transfer the batter into a squeeze bottle.

CREATE

Take your bottle of batter and make a circular shape for the head. Immediately start adding legs (eight, to be exact). You can take some creative freedom here and make them as squiggly and crazy as you want. Just be sure you add all eight legs, or else your daughter will call you out on it and give you a lecture about how it needs eight legs or it's not an octopus.

When your octopus has been flipped and is finished cooking on both sides, remove it from the heat.

PLATE

Place your octopus on the plate and add two chocolate chips for the eyes. Octo-goodness!

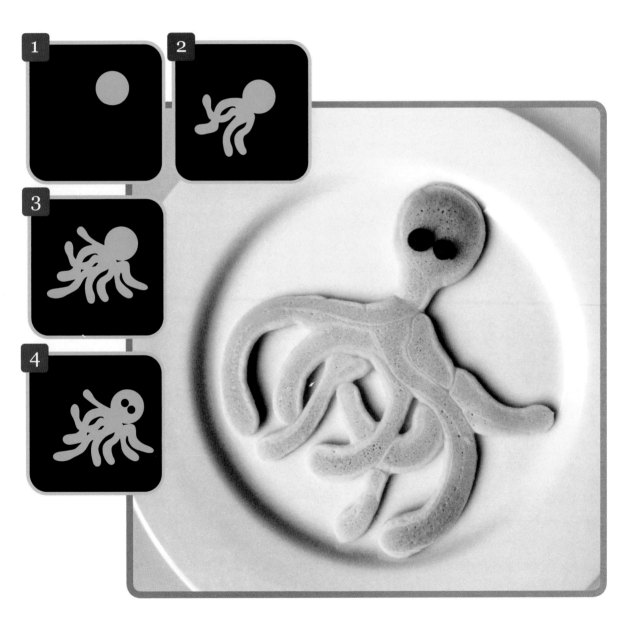

Mr. Pigsley

· ·

This little piggy went to market, and *this* little piggy went to breakfast . . . at your house! This is a pretty simple but fun pancake.

PREPARATION

For this recipe, you will need:

- Plain pancake batter
- Natural red food coloring
- One squeeze bottle (or plastic bag; see page 8)
- Chocolate chips

Color all of the batter with red food coloring, adding just enough to make your batter pink. Transfer the batter into a squeeze bottle.

CREATE

Let's start with the outline of the pig. As you see in the illustration, the pig is made up of circles, with two triangles for ears and one squiggle for the tail. When you have all your shapes outlined, fill them in.

Once Mr. Pigsley (this is the name I gave him—you can call your pig whatever you want) is fully cooked on both sides, carefully remove from the heat.

PLATE

Place the pig on your plate with the tail under the body, sticking out just a bit. Then put the head on top of the body. Add the legs, the nose, and two chocolate chips for eyes, and "pig" out!

Turtle

· ·

You won't have to "shell" out money to make this turtle!

PREPARATION

For this recipe, you will need:

- Plain pancake batter
- Natural green food coloring
- Natural brown food coloring (optional)
- Two or three squeeze bottles (or plastic bags; see page 8)
- Chocolate chips

Split the batter into two equal parts in two separate bowls. Add green food coloring to one portion; leave the other plain. (If using brown batter, a tiny amount will suffice.) Transfer the batter into separate squeeze bottles.

CREATE

First cook three small round pancakes with plain batter—the support for the turtle's shell.

Next, with the green batter, draw the outline and internal pattern of the shell. (You may use brown batter for the internal pattern.) Let it cook for a few moments so it will be darker. As always, watch the batter! Now fill in the shell with the green batter. Cook it lightly to keep the color lighter. Flip the shell and move it to the side.

Using the plain batter, make the four feet, small round pancakes. Draw a quick line on the griddle for the tail, and draw the head in the shape of a teardrop.

PLATE

First, set the feet on the plate. Next, stack the three small round pancakes one atop another. Form the shell on the stack of pancakes and set it atop the feet. You may have to use force to squish it to form. It's a turtle shell, after all, so it should survive. Add the head and the tail, with chocolate chips for the eyes.

Remember, slow and steady wins the race!

Frog

· ·

The only thing wrong with this little guy is that he can't jump into your mouth for you. You will still have to use your fork (or hands if you are in a hurry).

PREPARATION

For this recipe, you will need:

- Plain pancake batter
- Natural green food coloring
- One squeeze bottle (or plastic bag; see page 8)
- Chocolate chips

Split the batter into two parts in two separate bowls, one portion large and the other tiny, for just the eyes. Add green food coloring to the larger portion and leave the smaller portion plain. Transfer the green batter to a squeeze bottle, and set the plain portion aside.

CREATE

We'll begin with the head and body. Take the green pancake batter and outline an oval and a funny-shaped frog head. You can also add a mouth inside the frog head at the same time if you want to give him a special expression. Let the outlines cook for a moment, then fill them in. Let the head and body cook for a moment before flipping them. Cook thoroughly, then set them aside.

Next you want to create the frog legs. You can create two similar sets or you can go crazy and create four different legs to place with your frog. Take the green pancake batter and draw thin arms and hands. Let them cook for a moment, then remove them.

With the plain pancake batter, create two small dots. These dots will be used to create the frog's eyes. Let the eyes cook for a moment, then remove them.

PLATE

Set the legs down first, then place the frog body on top. Put the frog head on top of the body. Place the eyes on the frog and then top each of them with a chocolate chip.

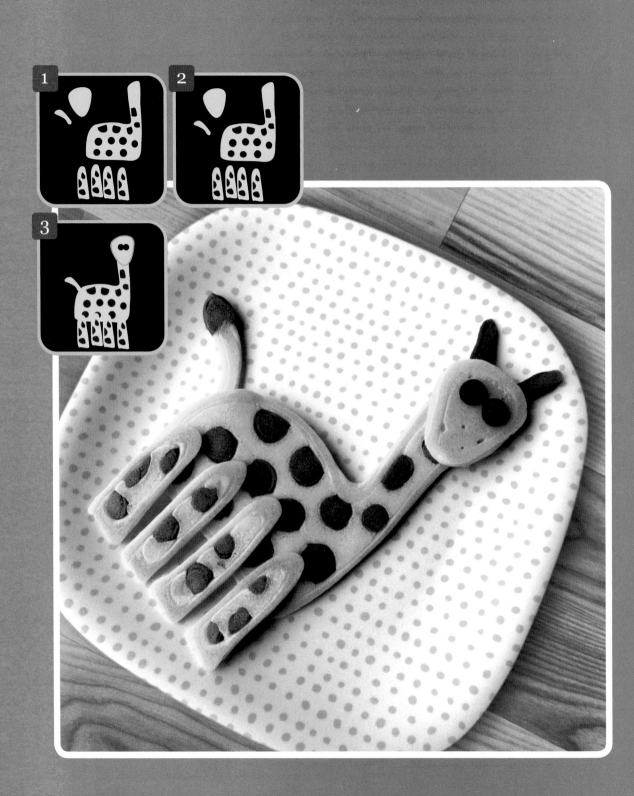

Giraffe

As a cheap alternative to going on safari, you can create these giraffes in the wild. Or in the kitchen, which probably is easier.

PREPARATION

For this recipe, you will need:

- Plain pancake batter
- Natural yellow food coloring
- Natural brown food coloring
- Two squeeze bottles (or plastic bags; see page 8)
- Chocolate chips

Split the batter into two parts in two separate bowls, one portion about four times larger than the other. Add yellow food coloring to the smaller portion; this will serve as the outline for your giraffe. Add brown food coloring to the other portion for the details. Transfer the batter into two separate squeeze bottles.

CREATE

First, draw the outlines of the giraffe, including the body, head, tail, and legs, with the yellow batter. Fill the body and legs with intersecting lines. The space you create will allow you to fill these in later with the brown batter. Let the outline sit for a few moments, cooking it thoroughly. Fill in the head completely.

After letting the outline cook for about 30 seconds to retain its shape, fill in the rest of the body and legs with the brown batter. Also use the brown batter to put an end on the tail and make the giraffe's two horns. Let the batter cook for a little while before flipping the giraffe. Let it cook a little more before plating it.

PLATE

Place the tail on the plate, set the body down gently, and place the head and legs overlapping the body. Add chocolate chips for eyes and devour the giraffe like a lion on the Serengeti would. Lions use syrup, right?

For the 3-D Version

CREATE

First, draw the outlines of the giraffe's body, head, and legs with the yellow batter, as shown in the illustrations. When you fill in the outlines, leave a few holes; you'll fill them in with brown batter for the giraffe's spots. Leave slots in each set of legs so they can support the body. If you've ever assembled a wooden dinosaur puzzle, it's the same concept.

Let the outlines sit for a few moments, then fill them, and fill the holes with the brown batter.

Flip the parts as soon as possible so that the yellow doesn't look burned or discolored. Once they are flipped, cook thoroughly. When creating 3-D pancakes, it's a good idea to cook them as long as possible (without burning!) to get a bit of a crispy shell. This will help the figure stand up and be more structurally sound.

PLATE

Once the parts are finished cooking and are a little stiff to the touch, assemble them. Place the two leg sets on the plate vertically. An extra pair of hands helps (usually Allie holds the legs for me). Next, insert the body into the slots. It may take a little trial and error for the giraffe to stand perfectly. Move the legs forward and backward to find a balance point. Finally, attach the head. "Glue" it on with a bit of batter: Apply a few drips to the back of the head and join it to the neck, then cook the batter with a torch. Alternatively, cake-decorating icing works great as glue.

Unicorn

· ·

No longer a myth, these creatures are easy to capture, or in this case, to create. Nothing mystical here, just pure deliciousness!

PREPARATION

For this recipe, you will need:

- Plain pancake batter
- Natural red food coloring
- Natural brown food coloring
- Natural yellow food coloring
- Four squeeze bottles (or plastic bags; see page 8)
- Chocolate chips

Split the batter into four parts in four separate bowls, with one part about twice as big as each of the other three. The largest portion will be left plain. Add red food coloring to one of the remaining portions, brown food coloring to another, and yellow to the last one. Transfer the batter into four separate squeeze bottles.

CREATE

Start with the general outline of a horse and let it cook for a few minutes. Also create the horn. After that, take your red batter and create the outline of the hair and the tail. Then take the brown pancake batter and create the hooves. As soon as you complete the hooves, come back with your plain pancake batter and fill in the body. Use the yellow (or whatever color you wish) to complete the hair and tail.

PLATE

There truly isn't anything mystical about the plating of this creature. Just lay the unicorn gently onto the plate, put the horn on top, place chocolate chips for the eyes, add your syrup, and enjoy. Watch out for the horn!

Flamingo

· ·

What's better than a lawn flamingo? A plate flamingo! A stylish, tasty pick-me-up for breakfast.

PREPARATION

For this recipe, you will need:

- Plain pancake batter
- Natural red food coloring
- Natural brown food coloring
- Three squeeze bottles (or plastic bags; see page 8)
- Chocolate chips

Split the batter into three parts in three separate bowls, with about three-fourths of the batter in one bowl, and equal smaller amounts in each of the other bowls. Add red food coloring to the larger portion to make a pink color. Add brown to one of the smaller portions. Leave the last portion plain. Transfer the batter into three separate squeeze bottles.

CREATE

Begin with the pink batter and start making the shapes for the flamingo's body. Fill those shapes in.

Now let's give our flamingo a beak! With your plain batter, make a small white strip, attaching it to the head. Then, with your brown batter, make the rest of the beak.

On the side of the griddle, make a small circle with the plain batter that you will use for the eye.

When they are finished cooking, remove all pieces from the heat.

PLATE

Place the body on the plate. Then add the legs, wing, and eye. Give him an eyeball with a chocolate chip, and there is your flamingo! It's like Florida, for breakfast.

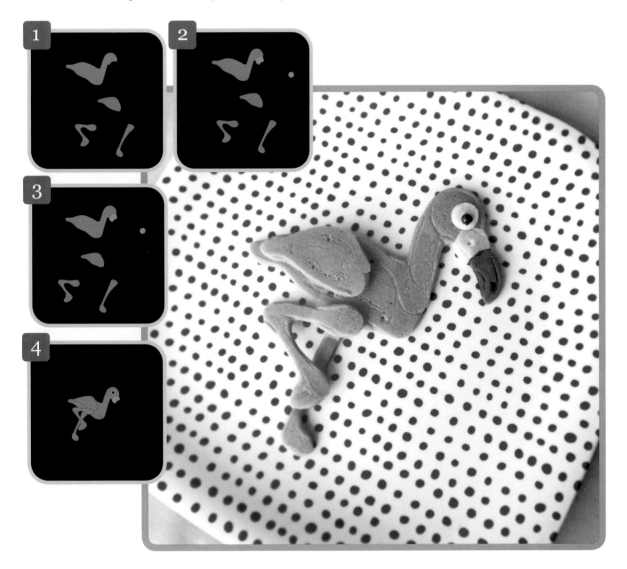

Butterfly

You'll be yearning for grassy meadows and sunlit skies when you create this wonderful pancake.

PREPARATION

For this recipe, you will need:

- Plain pancake batter
- Natural brown food coloring (or another color, if you want)
- Natural red food coloring (or another color, if you want)
- Two or three squeeze bottles (or plastic bags; see page 8)

You're using either two or three squeeze bottles, depending on the coloring of your butterfly. You can use whatever colors you like. Split the batter into two or three equal parts in separate bowls and add your favorite coloring to each portion. The last bit is to remain plain. Transfer the batter into separate squeeze bottles.

CREATE

For this creation, you'll have to choose a few different colors. You'll also use a portion of the batter to mix for the outline. Create the outline of the butterfly body first, using the brown batter, and let it cook thoroughly. It's almost like you're creating larger circles on top of smaller ones. Flip the outline of the body and then fill it in. Don't forget to include the antennae for the head!

Next, we'll do the wings. Outline the butterfly wings with the red batter. After that, go back to the plain batter and fill in some small round pancakes within the frame of the wings, or whatever other design you'd like for the wings. Fill in the rest of the wings with the red batter and cook it thoroughly on both sides.

After a few moments, the butterfly should be ready to plate.

PLATE

If you have a nearby sunflower or springlike plant, you could rest your butterfly on it for the ultimate presentation. If not, it looks great on a plate, too!

Snake

· ·

This is probably the only time you'll be allowing a snake on the breakfast table.

PREPARATION

For this recipe, you will need:

- Plain pancake batter
- Natural green food coloring
- Natural red food coloring
- Two squeeze bottles (or plastic bags; see page 8)
- Chocolate chips

Split the batter into two parts in two separate bowls, with the majority in one bowl and a tiny amount in the other bowl, just for the tongue. Add green food coloring to the larger portion and red food coloring to the other. Transfer the batter into two separate squeeze bottles.

CREATE

For the snake's body, make a big spiral with the batter. Gradually let the body get thinner as you get closer to the tail. On the side, make the snake's head in a simple teardrop shape.

Get your red batter out now and make the snake's tongue. A simple forked shape will do.

Remove all the pieces from the heat.

PLATE

Overlap the coil of the snake to add some dimension. Next, add the tongue, the head, and a couple of chocolate chips for eyes. It's time to strike and dig in!

Bluebird

There's a bluebird on my shoulder, or wait, I think he's on my plate. Impress your kids with some 3-D pancake action.

PREPARATION

For this recipe, you will need:

- Plain pancake batter
- Natural blue food coloring
- Natural yellow food coloring
- Natural brown food coloring
- Two squeeze bottles (or plastic bags; see page 8)

Split the batter into three parts in three separate bowls. You'll need more than half of the batter blue, and the yellow part will be smaller. You will need only a tiny amount of brown, for the eye. Transfer the blue and yellow batters into two separate squeeze bottles. The brown batter can be set aside.

CREATE

Start with the blue batter to make the body of the bird, forming the bottom portion first. You will need to leave an opening for the rest of the bird to slide into later on.

Next, make the main part of the bird's body, leaving a small open circle for the eye. Fill in the open circle with the brown batter. Add a yellow triangle beak to the body. Do this while the body is still cooking so they will be cooked together.

Set those pieces aside and use the yellow batter to make your bird's feet, as shown in the illustrations. You will not flip these. Let the batter start bubbling. Before it sets, take the bottom portion of the bird (the legs) and stand it upright across the two feet. As the yellow batter cooks, it will hold the blue portion up on its own.

PLATE

Carefully remove the bottom portion from the heat and transfer it to your plate. Now take the top portion of the bird and place it in the slot you made in the bottom portion. This bluebird may not sing, but it sure tastes good!

Monkey Face

Boys and girls alike will enjoy a monkey on their plate. You might even get them to eat some bananas.

PREPARATION

For this recipe, you will need:

- Plain pancake batter
- Natural brown food coloring
- Natural red food coloring
- Three squeeze bottles (or plastic bags; see page 8)
- Chocolate chips

Split the batter into three parts in three separate bowls, just under three-fourths in one, under one-fourth in another, and the last, tiny amount in the third bowl. Add brown food coloring to the largest portion, keep the next one plain, and add red food coloring to the smallest. Transfer the batter into three separate squeeze bottles.

CREATE

For this pancake, we will be playing with cooking times. We'll start with the outline of your monkey's head. You may want to try it out on paper first to get a feel for it. For the top, make an upside-down U shape with the brown batter. Now, with the plain batter, make outlines for the jaw and the ears. Make a smile inside the jaw with the red batter.

Fill in the ears and the rest of the jaw with plain batter. Then draw two ovals with plain batter inside the upside-down U, for the eyes. Fill in around the eyes with brown batter.

Once the face is finished cooking, remove it from the heat.

PLATE

Put your monkey face on the plate, and don't forget the eyes! Place two chocolate chips on the eyeballs. Today it's okay to monkey around at breakfast.

Whale

· ·

There she blows! Do some whale watching . . . from the table!

PREPARATION

For this recipe, you will need:

- Plain pancake batter
- Natural blue food coloring (or another color, if you like)
- One squeeze bottle (or plastic bag; see page 8)
- Chocolate chips

Split the pancake batter into two parts in two separate bowls. One bowl will have the majority of the batter, for the blue food coloring. Leave only a tiny amount plain. Transfer the colored batter to a squeeze bottle, and set the plain portion aside.

CREATE

With the blue batter, make the shape of the whale. On the side you can make the water spurt to spruce it up. Now, with your plain batter, make a little circle for the eye on the side. Flip it quickly to keep the color light.

When your whale piece is done, remove it from the heat.

PLATE

Place the whale body on the plate. Add the eye and the water spurt. The last touch is a chocolate chip for the eye. A pancake so good I bet they'll eat the "whale" thing!

Ducks

· ·

The most quacktastic pancakes you'll find in this book.

PREPARATION

For this recipe, you will need:

- Plain pancake batter
- Natural yellow food coloring
- Natural orange food coloring
- Three squeeze bottles (or plastic bags; see page 8)
- Chocolate chips

Split the batter into three parts in three separate bowls, one about three-fourths of the total, and the other two smaller portions equal. Add yellow food coloring to the large portion, and orange food coloring to one of the smaller portions, and leave the other smaller portion plain. Transfer the batter into three separate squeeze bottles.

CREATE

With the yellow batter, create an outline of the large duck, then fill it in. Take the orange batter and add the duck's bill to the body. Cook thoroughly and set aside.

Next, outline the duck's wing with the yellow batter, then fill it in; cook it thoroughly and set it aside.

Then create the ducklings. You will want to make a body that is similar to the larger duck's wing, but with a round head. Quickly add an orange bill to each of the ducklings, and let them cook until they are ready to flip. After cooking on the other side, remove and set aside.

Use the plain batter to create a dot for the main duck's eye. Remove and set aside.

PLATE

Set your larger duck's body on a plate and place the wing on top, near the center. Take the plain-batter dot and place it as the eye, then put a chocolate chip on top. Arrange the ducklings to look like they are following the larger duck, and give each of them a smaller bit of chocolate broken off from a chocolate chip for an eye.

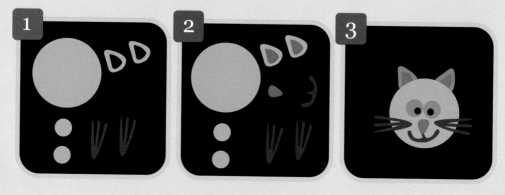

Cat Face

- -

Naturally, this is just a purr-fect dish to create!

PREPARATION

For this recipe, you will need:

- Plain pancake batter
- Natural brown food coloring
- Natural red food coloring
- Three squeeze bottles (or plastic bags; see page 8)
- Chocolate chips

Split the pancake batter into three parts in three separate bowls, one portion about three-fourths of the batter, and the other two smaller, equal portions. Add the brown and red food coloring to each of the two smaller portions. Leave the other portion plain. Transfer the batter into three separate squeeze bottles.

CREATE

Starting with the plain batter, make a regular round pancake. Set aside.

Now start working on the ears. Keeping with the plain batter, create two small triangle outlines; use your red batter to fill the triangles. Let the outline and the triangles cook a little. Staying with the red batter, lay down another small triangle on the griddle. This will be the cat's nose. Set it aside and start forming the mouth with the brown batter.

The mouth will be in the shape of an anchor or a wishbone, depending on what you want your cat's mood to be!

After finishing the mouth, cook two small pancakes with the plain batter for the eyes. Don't forget to lay down two larger W pancakes with the brown batter, to serve as the whiskers. Let them cook for a few moments, and then you're ready for plating.

PLATE

First, lay down the larger plain pancake and the ears. Put the two small plain-batter pancakes for the eyes near the center of the larger pancake, and the red triangle just below them near the center. Take the mouth and set it right below the red triangle. Take the two W's and set them next to the nose to create the whiskers. Then take two chocolate chips and set them on the eyes, and there you have it! Pet accordingly or eat accordingly, it's all up to you!

Sheep

· ·

There's no need to pull the wool over anyone's eyes here! This pancake is "shear" bliss!

PREPARATION

For this recipe, you will need:

• Plain pancake batter

• Natural brown food coloring

• Two squeeze bottles (or plastic bags; see page 8)

• Chocolate chips

Split the batter into two parts in two separate bowls, with one portion about four times larger than the other. Keep the larger portion plain, and add brown food coloring to the smaller portion. Transfer the batter into two separate squeeze bottles.

CREATE

We'll start with the wool. To make it, imagine you're outlining a fluffy cloud with the plain pancake batter. Then fill in the wool/cloud and set it aside.

Using the brown batter, create the head of the sheep, laying down a small, rounded triangle. Don't forget to add the ears for the sheep as well. Also lay down four thin strips of brown pancake batter to serve as the legs. Let them cook for a moment, then remove them from the heat.

PLATE

Position the four legs, and then gently place the wool over them as in the illustration; then put the head in place. Use two chocolate chips to serve as the eyes, and enjoy. Just don't make too many sheep and start counting them. They could put you right back to sleep!

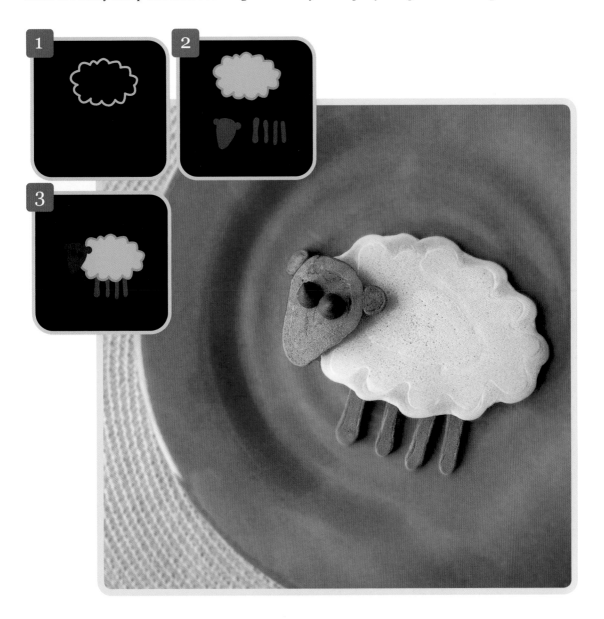

Bug

. . . .

Bugs are pests in most cases. But in this case, they're delicious pests. You can play the role of exterminator here!

PREPARATION

For this recipe, you will need:

- Plain pancake batter
- Natural brown food coloring
- One squeeze bottle (or plastic bag; see page 8)
- Lighter
- Chocolate chips

Color all of the pancake batter with brown food coloring. Transfer the batter to a squeeze bottle.

CREATE

The tricky part of this project is not the pieces, but attaching them patiently, properly, and precisely to make the bug stand in 3-D. Start with the legs by laying out four curved lines. Cook them thoroughly, as they will serve to hold up the body of the bug, along with its head. Don't overcook them, though, as you don't want to lose the flavor.

Next, work on the body, which is just a small oval pancake. Then make the head, which is a smaller round shape. Cook both pieces and set them aside.

Here's the tricky part, and where your patience comes in.

Take each of the legs and attach it to the body. To do this, you'll have to use the extra batter and a lighter to cook the batter. The extra batter will serve as the "glue." First, find a way to prop up the body on its side. Take one of the legs and attach it to the body using the extra batter. Then take the lighter and cook the batter, making sure the leg cooks into the body. Repeat this process for the rest of the legs.

After attaching the legs, stand up the body to test its stability. Hopefully it'll have some legs to stand on!

Now your bug body should be standing on its own well enough so you can attach the head. You don't have to prop up the body this time if it's standing on its own. Just use more "glue" and attach the head with the lighter. If you've angled the head correctly, you'll be able to place the chocolate chip eyes on top once you've plated the bug.

PLATE

Gently place the bug on the plate. Douse this critter in syrup so it won't crawl away!

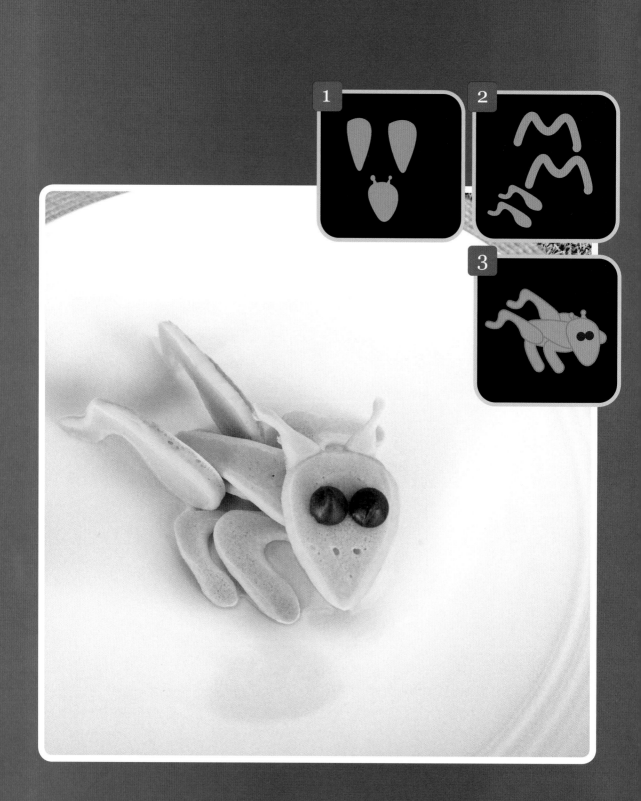

Grasshopper

. . . .

Now, young grasshopper, it's time to sharpen your skills with another insect pancake. This fellow won't hop away!

PREPARATION

For this recipe, you will need:

- Plain pancake batter
- Natural green food coloring
- One squeeze bottle (or plastic bag; see page 8)
- Lighter
- Chocolate chips

Color all of the batter with green food coloring. Transfer the batter into a squeeze bottle.

CREATE

Like the other 3-D pieces, the tricky part of this project is not the pieces themselves, but attaching them patiently, properly, and precisely to make it stand as a 3-D pancake.

Start with the body, which is an elongated triangle. Then make the head, which is more of an egg shape. The antennae, pointy small triangles, are attached to the head.

Next make the legs. These will be rather thick, but you still need to cook them well, as they will hold up the body of the grasshopper, along with its head. Don't overcook them, though—you don't want them to turn brown. The rear legs of the grasshopper are shaped like L's, while the two sets of forelegs are shaped like rounded M's.

Now for the tricky part. Let's work the forelegs first, which are easier; you can lay the body of the grasshopper on top of them. It's the rear legs that you'll have to pay more attention to. With the picture as a guide, attach the legs to the side of the body using the extra batter "glue" and the lighter. Make sure the legs and body can stand on their own.

After attaching the legs, stand up the body to test its stability. Obviously, we're hoping for it to stand!

The grasshopper is now ready for its head. Use more batter glue and attach the head with the lighter. Angle the head slightly so that you can place the chocolate chips on top to serve as eyes once you've plated the grasshopper.

PLATE

Gently place your grasshopper on the plate, and give him chocolate chip eyes. Pour on syrup so he won't hop away!

Snail

. . . .

Snails are known as a delicacy in certain parts of the world, and this snail is no exception, though it's probably sweeter. And much cuter!

PREPARATION

For this recipe, you will need:

- Plain pancake batter
- Natural brown food coloring
- Natural green food coloring
- Three squeeze bottles (or plastic bags; see page 8)
- Chocolate chips

Split the batter into three parts in three separate bowls, with one portion a tiny amount, the next portion about three-fourths of the remaining batter, and the third portion whatever remains. Leave the smallest portion plain, add enough brown food coloring to the largest portion to make it rather dark, and color the third portion green. Transfer the batter into three separate squeeze bottles.

CREATE

We'll start with the shell. Take the brown pancake batter and make a swirl pattern, like a lollipop. Let the shell cook for a moment, then fill in the area around the swirl. Cook it thoroughly and set it aside.

The body of the snail is simple. Create two small pancakes using the plain pancake batter as the eyes, and run a line of green pancake batter from the eyes to what will be the body of the snail. The body of the snail is best described as a horizontal L. Use the illustration as a guide to create your snail body. You could even use the brown batter to make a tiny smile for your snail if you're so inclined. You will be ready to plate the snail after letting it cook for a few minutes.

PLATE

Set the snail body on the plate first, making sure to be gentle with the placement, as the eyes of the snail are connected in a rather fragile way to the body. Next, take the shell and lay it over the longer part of the snail's body. Add two chocolate chips for the eyes, and voilà—a snail fit for a fancy dinner party!

Spider and Spiderweb

A great pancake for any arachnophile—or a great way to help people overcome their arachnophobia.

PREPARATION

For this recipe, you will need:

- Plain pancake batter
- Natural brown food coloring
- Two squeeze bottles (or plastic bags; see page 8)

Split the batter into two equal parts in two separate bowls. Add brown food coloring to one of the portions and leave the other portion plain. Transfer the batter into two separate squeeze bottles.

CREATE

With the brown batter, create a little spider. Start with a slightly oval body and then add the legs and fangs (the spider might not be large enough to accommodate a full set of legs). Let the spider cook and set it aside for later.

Next create the spider's web for the little guy to rest on. Take the plain pancake batter and start with a thin, small circle in the middle of your griddle, then draw some lines that extend out from the circle.

Finally, in each segment between the lines, create two reverse arches to give it the full spiderweb effect. Let the web cook just long enough for it to stay solid and connected. Be careful when flipping or removing the web.

PLATE

Set your spiderweb on a plate and place the spider on top of the web. Try to keep the flies away (unless those flies are made out of pancake batter).

Dinosaur

Though this may look rather complicated, if you follow the instructions and use a little know-how, it should be a walk in the Jurassic Park.

PREPARATION

For this recipe, you will need:

- Plain pancake batter
- Natural green food coloring
- Natural brown food coloring
- Two squeeze bottles (or plastic bags; see page 8)
- Chocolate chips

Split the batter into two parts in two separate bowls, about twice as much in one as in the other. Add green food coloring to the larger portion and brown to the smaller. Transfer the batter into two separate squeeze bottles.

CREATE

Start by drawing the outline of the body and head with the green batter. Fill it in, but leave a few areas along the spine of the dinosaur for spots. Next, draw four stubby legs and let them cook. After the body cooks for about 30 seconds to a minute, add the brown batter in the empty areas to fill in the spots. Flip all pieces and let them cook thoroughly.

PLATE

Place the body on the plate first, then add the legs on top. Finally, add a chocolate chip for the eye.

For the 3-D Version

CREATE

First, draw the outline of the dinosaur's body, head, and legs, as shown in the illustrations. When you fill in the outline, leave a few holes in the design; you'll fill them in with brown batter for the dinosaur's spots. When you make the legs, leave a slot in each set so that they can support the body. If you've ever assembled a wooden dinosaur puzzle, it's the same concept.

Let the outlines sit for a few moments, then fill them, and fill the holes with the brown batter.

Flip the parts as soon as possible so that the "good side" doesn't look burned or discolored. Once they are flipped, cook thoroughly. When making 3-D pancakes, it's a good idea to cook them as long as possible (without burning!) to get a bit of a crispy shell. This will help the figure stand up and be more structurally sound.

PLATE

Once the parts are finished cooking and are a little stiff to the touch, it's time to assemble them. Place the two leg sets on the plate vertically. An extra pair of hands is a big help at this point; it's a great job for the kiddos. Next, insert the body into the slots. It may take a little trial and error to get the pieces to stand perfectly. Move the legs forward and backward to find a nice balance point.

6

PANCAKE FOOD

Tacos

This one is also assembled in parts, just like a true taco!

PREPARATION

For this recipe, you will need:

- Plain pancake batter
- Natural red food coloring
- Natural yellow food coloring
- Natural green food coloring
- Natural brown food coloring
- Five squeeze bottles (or plastic bags; see page 8)

Put about half of the plain batter into a squeeze bottle, and divide the rest into four equal portions. Add red food coloring to one of the smaller portions, green to another, yellow to another, and brown to the last. Transfer the colored batter into four separate squeeze bottles.

CREATE

Start by making the tortilla shell, an oval shape, with the plain pancake batter. Next, work on the meat, which you'll create as an irregularly shaped half-moon, using the brown pancake batter to simulate the pork, beef, or whatever you fancy! The tomatoes and lettuce are created by laying down the green and red in spikes. Don't forget the cheese: I usually draw a yellow squiggly line with yellow for this.

PLATE

Not too much to do for plating, as this is a handheld food! Just fold the "tortilla shell" in half and place the meat, lettuce, tomatoes, and cheese inside the shell.

Hot sauce or salsa is optional, though if you like spice in your pancakes, you should go for it!

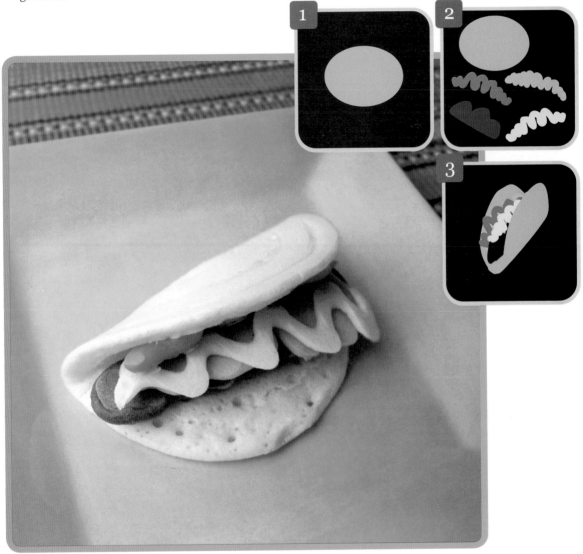

Bacon 'n' Eggs

Though I'm partial to the actual thing, this just serves as a fun alternative. I do miss the sound of sizzling bacon, though.

PREPARATION

For this recipe, you will need:

- Plain pancake batter
- Natural yellow food coloring
- Natural red food coloring
- Four squeeze bottles (or plastic bags; see page 8)

Split the batter into four equal parts in four separate bowls. Add yellow food coloring to one part, red to another, and just enough red to another to make it pink; leave the last part plain. Transfer the batter into four separate squeeze bottles.

CREATE

First make a couple of circles with the yellow batter for the yolks. It's okay if you let them cook for a while, as the yellow takes a while to darken in color.

Next, make larger circles with plain batter for the egg whites. Cook them for a minimum amount of time on one side so that they remain as white as possible. Flip them over and continue to cook all the way through.

Now we'll make the "meaty" part of the bacon, using the red batter. Draw a couple of squiggly lines close enough to each other to almost touch. Let them cook for a few seconds, then fill in the gap and one edge with the pink batter for the bacon fat (Allie told me that "fat" is not a nice word, so maybe we'll call it "husky bacon"). Flip it over when bubbles appear in the batter. Instant pancake bacon!

When they are cooked, remove all pieces from the heat.

PLATE

Grab your plate and place the egg whites on the bottom and the yolks on top. Add a side of bacon and you're all set!

Cheeseburger and Fries

. . . .

Aside from apple pie, nothing is as all-American as a cheeseburger and fries. Especially if they're in pancake form!

PREPARATION

For this recipe, you will need:

- Plain pancake batter
- Natural yellow food coloring
- Natural red food coloring
- Natural green food coloring
- Natural brown food coloring
- Five squeeze bottles (or plastic bags; see page 8)

Split the batter into five equal parts in five separate bowls. Add yellow food coloring to one portion, red to the second, green to the third, and brown to the fourth; leave the last part plain. Transfer the batter into five separate squeeze bottles.

CREATE

Let's begin with the bun. Make two simple circle shapes with the plain batter. To add some dimension to the top bun, add a lot of batter quickly. This makes for a fluffier pancake.

Next, let's make the pieces that go between the buns. For the cheese, make a square with the yellow batter. Start with the edges, then fill in the rest. Try to keep the remaining pieces similar in size, as you will be stacking them at the end.

The hamburger patty is a circle made with the brown batter. The tomato is a slightly smaller circle made with the red batter. For the lettuce, make a squiggly shape with the green batter and fill it in. The mustard is just a quick squiggle with the yellow batter.

Now let's make the fries. Take your yellow batter and make a few lines of various sizes. You'll probably want to make a lot of fries, because they are pretty popular. Allie likes to "taste-test" them to be sure they are okay. You can then make a shape like a french fries box, and/or a puddle of ketchup, with the red batter.

When they're done, remove all the pieces from the heat.

PLATE

The fun part is building the cheeseburger. Start with the bottom bun and layer on up. Arrange the fries and top with the box and/or the ketchup. The healthiest fast-food breakfast you can get!

Spaghetti

· ·

This is a fun twist on a traditional classic that any kid is bound to appreciate. It is also quite simple, so it's a win-win.

PREPARATION

For this recipe, you will need:

- Plain pancake batter
- Natural red food coloring
- Two squeeze bottles (or plastic bags; see page 8)

Split the batter into two equal parts in two separate bowls. Add red food coloring to one part and leave the other plain. Transfer the batter into two separate squeeze bottles.

CREATE

Start with the plain batter and have fun. Make some squiggly lines, trying to keep within a somewhat circular area. Vary the size so you can layer them to add dimension. These are great pancakes for the kids to help out with—the more squiggly the lines, the better!

For the meatballs, make some red circles and fill them in. You can cook them a little longer to get a brownish tint.

When they are finished cooking, remove all the pieces from the heat.

PLATE

Layer and intermix the squiggly lines, add the red circles, and now you have spaghetti for breakfast. Pasta never tasted so sweet—unless you eat your pasta with syrup. Gross.

Watermelon

· ·

Enjoy a summer favorite all year round. No fear of watermelons growing in your belly if you eat these seeds!

PREPARATION

For this recipe, you will need:

- Plain pancake batter
- Natural red food coloring
- Natural green food coloring
- Three squeeze bottles (or plastic bags; see page 8)
- Chocolate chips

Split the batter into three parts in three separate bowls, with one portion about two-thirds of the batter, and the rest divided equally. Add red food coloring to this largest portion, add green to one of the smaller portions, and leave the other small portion plain. Transfer the batter into three separate squeeze bottles.

CREATE

Start with the watermelon rind, which basically is just a big green smile. Add a stripe of plain batter to the inside of the rind.

Next, let's fill in the red. When the watermelon is ripe and cooked, remove it from the heat.

PLATE

Put the watermelon on the plate, add chocolate chip seeds, and enjoy. Perhaps you can fetch some lemonade for the full effect!

Lollipop

· ·

Finally, a lollipop that won't give you cavities.

PREPARATION

For this recipe, you will need:

- Plain pancake batter
- Natural red food coloring
- Natural yellow food coloring
- Natural blue food coloring
- Four squeeze bottles (or plastic bags; see page 8)

Split the batter into four equal parts in four separate bowls. Add the colors to three of the portions and leave one plain. Transfer the batter into four separate squeeze bottles.

CREATE

You can take some creative freedom on this and order the colors as you like. To follow the example here, start with your red batter. Make a large swirling circle, keeping in mind that you will be adding the other colors. On the side, with your plain batter, make the lollipop stick.

Next, get your blue batter and follow the red swirl, starting in the middle. You can make this swirl thicker. Now add a swirl with the yellow batter. Fill in the rest of the space with the yellow too. You can outline the circle with the red batter if you want.

Once everything is cooked through, remove it from the heat.

PLATE

Lay the lollipop stick on your plate and add the circle to the top. Who says you can't have candy for breakfast?

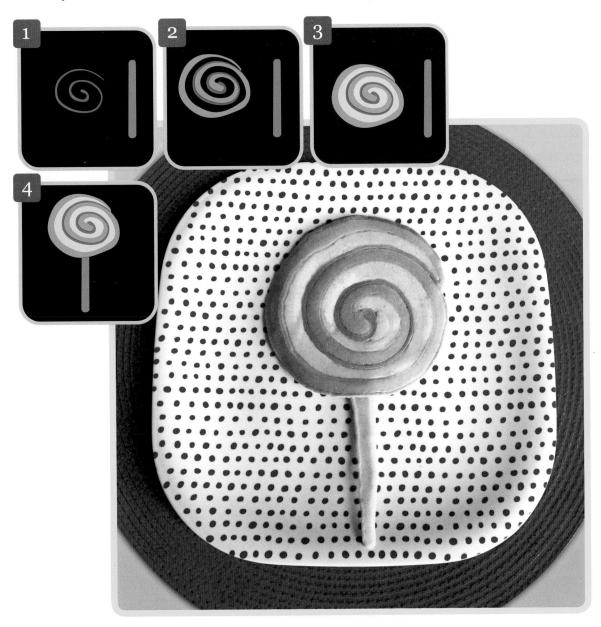

Ice Cream Cone

Dessert . . . for breakfast? This pancake is a fun way to start a hot day . . . or any day, for that matter.

PREPARATION

For this recipe, you will need:

- Plain pancake batter
- Natural brown food coloring
- Natural red food coloring
- Natural yellow food coloring
- Four squeeze bottles (or plastic bags; see page 8)

Split the batter into four equal parts in four separate bowls. Add the colors to three of the parts and leave one plain. Transfer the batter into four separate squeeze bottles.

CREATE

Ice cream is always more fun in a cone, so let's start with that. Make a long triangle with your brown batter and fill it in.

On the side of the griddle, we will make our ice cream scoops. Make one scoop each with your red, yellow, and plain batters.

When your ice cream parts are done cooking (I never thought I'd be saying that), remove them from the heat.

PLATE

Starting with the cone, layer the pieces of the ice cream cone as shown in the illustration.
Time for ice cream—for breakfast.

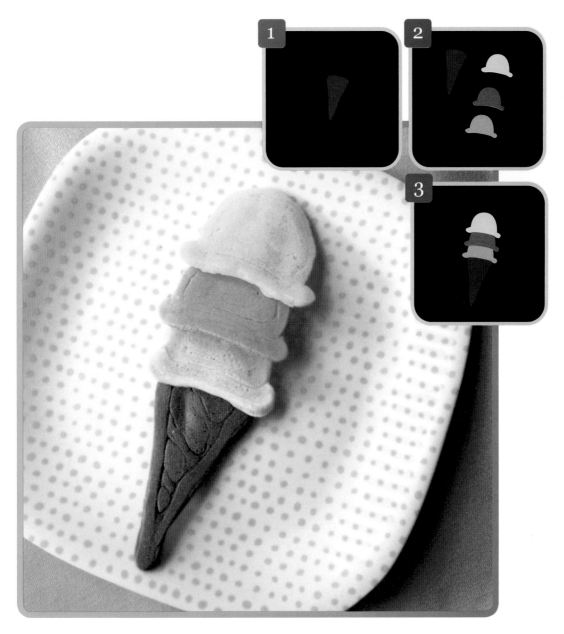

There's a Worm in My Apple!

An apple a day keeps the doctor away. I'd like to think that applies to apple pancakes as well.

PREPARATION

For this recipe, you will need:

- Plain pancake batter
- Natural green food coloring
- Natural brown food coloring
- Four squeeze bottles (or plastic bags; see page 8)
- Chocolate chips

Split the batter into four parts in four separate bowls. One part should be about a third of the batter. Divide the rest into three equal parts. Use that largest portion for the green food coloring. You will also make one of the smaller portions green, but with less food coloring, for a lighter shade. Add brown food coloring to another smaller portion and leave the last one plain. Transfer the batter into four separate squeeze bottles.

CREATE

Grab your darker green batter and make the outline of the apple. Fill it in, leaving a hole for the worm. With the plain batter, fill in part of the area that we made for the bite as shown.

With your lighter green batter, make your worm. I gave mine some ridges by making small circles. With the brown batter, make the stem for the apple.

When all pieces have cooked through on both sides, remove them from the heat.

PLATE

Lay your apple on the plate. Slip the stem under the top of the apple so it's sticking out. Fit the worm through the hole. Give him eyes with chocolate chips. Breakfast can now begin.

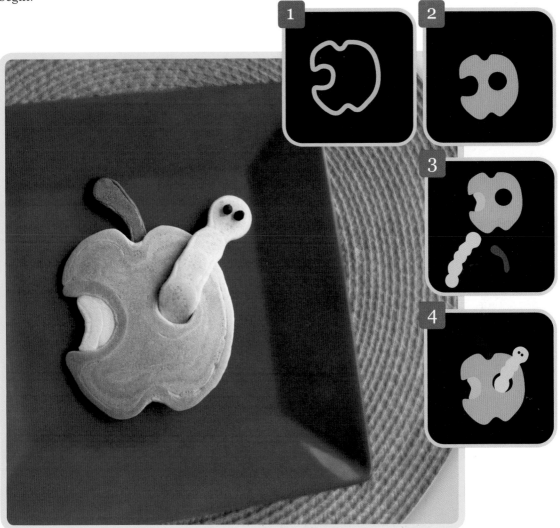

Sushi

. . . .

Allie hasn't had real sushi before; because of this creation, she thinks it's all made of pancakes.

PREPARATION

For this recipe, you will need:

- Plain pancake batter
- Natural green food coloring
- Natural red food coloring
- Natural blue food coloring
- Four squeeze bottles (or plastic bags; see page 8)

Split the batter into four equal parts in four separate bowls. Add the green, red, and blue food coloring, separately, in each of three of the portions. The fourth portion remains plain. Transfer the batter into four separate squeeze bottles.

CREATE

On the griddle, lay down a strip of the plain pancake batter 3 to 4 inches wide (7 to 10 centimeters for our metric folks). Then, pulling from the strip with a spatula, scrape the batter gently across the griddle to create a thin pancake. This will serve as the rice.

Next, take the squeeze bottle with blue batter and do the same, laying down a strip on the griddle and gently scraping it across. This will serve as the seaweed.

Now take the squeeze bottle with the red batter for some "salmon." Create a strip of pancake batter 3 to 4 inches wide, but do not scrape. Take the squeeze bottle with the green and do the same. I always like avocado in my sushi, so that's what this is.

These are the ingredients of our sushi platter.

PLATE

Before plating, you must roll the sushi into form. Using a cutting board, lay down the seaweed and then top with the layer of rice. Next take your other sushi ingredients, layer, and wrap! Cut it accordingly and plate it.

Chopsticks are optional. I'll leave it up to you to include the wasabi.

Birthday (Pan)Cake

· ·

What better way to start that special day than with a birthday pancake! This will make anyone's day, kids and adults alike.

PREPARATION

For this recipe, you will need:

- Plain pancake batter
- Natural red food coloring
- Natural yellow food coloring
- Four squeeze bottles (or plastic bags; see page 8)

Split the batter into four parts in four separate bowls. Place a third of the batter into one bowl, a third into another bowl, and divide the rest between two other bowls. Add red food coloring to one of the larger portions to make a nice red batter. Make the other larger portion pink by using less red food coloring. Leave one of the smaller portions plain, and add yellow to the other. Transfer the batter into four separate squeeze bottles.

CREATE

Start by making the cake portion. To do this, make four small pancakes with the red and pink batters. Once these are cooked, set them aside.

Make your candles with the yellow and plain batters—you can make as many candles as you like! The trick is to cook them just a bit longer so they will stand upright on your cake layers when they are finished.

Remove all the pieces from the heat.

PLATE

Stack your cake layers and make the appropriate number of slats in them with a butter knife or the handle end of a spoon. Stick your candles in the slats and it's party time!

Banana

· ·

Treat your little monkeys to banana pancakes. This is a really easy way to add some fun to breakfast.

PREPARATION

For this recipe, you will need:

- Plain pancake batter
- Natural yellow food coloring
- Two squeeze bottles (or plastic bags; see page 8)

Split the batter into two equal parts in two separate bowls. Add yellow food coloring to one portion and leave the other portion plain. Transfer the batter into two separate squeeze bottles.

CREATE

Let's start with the inner part of the banana, made with the plain batter. To keep it light-colored, make your pancake thin and flip it quickly. Cooking on a low temperature will help. Once it is flipped, you can let it cook all the way through—just the side you want facing up needs to remain light.

For the peel, grab your yellow batter and make the shapes you see in the illustrations.

Remove all the pieces from the heat.

PLATE

Lay the inner part of the banana down first, and then layer the peel pieces on top. Nothing goes to waste with these bananas!

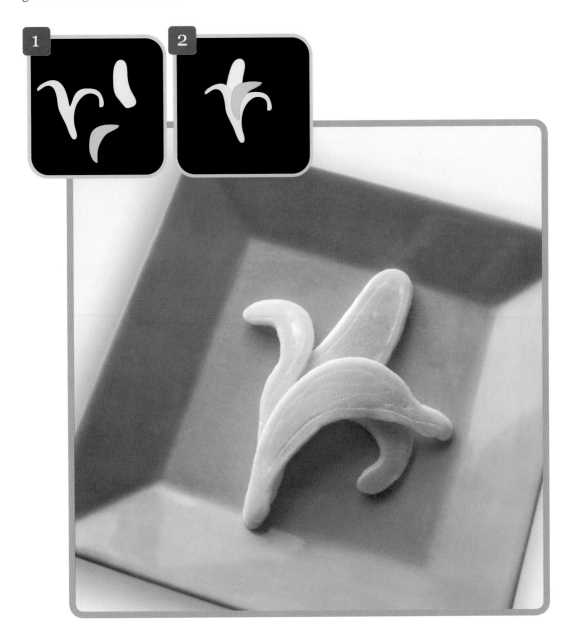

Salad

· ·

Though it's not exactly a health food, this pancake salad is still delicious, color-ful, and fun to eat.

PREPARATION

For this recipe, you will need:

- Plain pancake batter
- Natural green food coloring
- Natural yellow food coloring
- Natural red food coloring
- Four squeeze bottles (or plastic bags; see page 8)

Split the batter into four equal parts in four separate bowls. Add the colors to each of three of the parts and leave one plain. Transfer the batter into four separate squeeze bottles.

CREATE

This pancake creation requires the use of different colors and shapes to create the illusion of something healthy! Start by laying down some lettuce leaves with the green batter, beginning with the outlines and filling them in. Set them aside and prepare the tomatoes, which you will make as small red circles. Create as many as you'd like, and set them aside. Now use your yellow batter to create mini-pancake bean sprouts, and the plain batter to make croutons.

PLATE

You could set all of these pieces on a plate, but using a bowl would be better. Just throw in your salad ingredients, pour on your syrup dressing, toss, and enjoy!

Pancakes

· ·

Roll into your kitchen and order up a short stack of pancakes from the cook.

PREPARATION

For this recipe, you will need:

- Plain pancake batter
- Natural brown food coloring
- Natural yellow food coloring
- Three squeeze bottles (or plastic bags; see page 8)

Split the batter into three parts in three separate bowls, with one portion about three-fourths of the total, and the other two portions equal in size. Leave the large portion plain, and add brown food coloring to one of the smaller portions and yellow to the other. Transfer the batter into three separate squeeze bottles.

CREATE

First create two regular round pancakes with the plain batter (you can make more pancakes if you are super-hungry). Cook them and set them aside.

You can make the utensils if you are feeling extra artsy. Use whatever batter color you want to make the fork and knife handles. Quickly draw the letter E onto the fork handle and then a blade onto the knife handle. Remove the fork and knife once they have become stiff.

Next, make the syrup and butter. For the syrup, use the brown batter to draw a dot with wavy lines extending from it. For the butter, draw a square with the yellow batter and fill it in.

PLATE

Place the pancakes as the base and then put the brown syrup pancake on top of them. Then place the butter pancake on top of the syrup. If you made your own utensils, place them next to the pancakes and feel free to try to use them to eat your creation, because edible utensils mean less cleanup.

Pancake Cereal

This is one of the first "genius" ideas I had while I was making pancakes. It offers the convenience and flexible serving size of cereal and the sweetness of pancake batter. A definite win in my book!

PREPARATION

For this recipe, you will need:

- Plain pancake batter
- One squeeze bottle (or plastic bag; see page 8)

Transfer the batter into a squeeze bottle.

CREATE

This is one of the simplest pancake meals to create: Just lay down some tiny pancakes and cook them normally. You can choose to create them in different shapes—just keep it small and bite-size.

PLATE

Once the pancakes have finished cooking, don't use a plate. If you're doing this right, you're putting your tiny pancakes in a bowl and drenching them in syrup. No forks either! Use a spoon to create the authentic effect of eating cereal.

Side note: Young toddlers in particular really like this meal.

Hot Dog

· ·

Too cold to barbecue hot dogs outside? No problem, have them inside . . . for breakfast.

PREPARATION

For this recipe, you will need:

* Plain pancake batter
* Natural red food coloring
* Natural yellow food coloring
* Three squeeze bottles (or plastic bags; see page 8)

Split the batter into three parts in three separate bowls, making two larger portions, each a little more than a third of the batter, and one smaller portion. Add red food coloring to one of the larger portions and keep the other larger portion as plain pancake batter. Color the smaller portion with yellow. Transfer the batter into three separate squeeze bottles.

CREATE

This meal is assembled in pieces, starting with the bun. Using your plain pancake batter, lay down two elongated oval pancakes. Just think of the shape of hot dog buns and take it from there. After letting the batter cook for a few moments, flip it over, let it cook a few moments longer, and set it aside. Using the red batter, squeeze out another elongated oval, about the same length as the bun; this will be your frank. Cook that and set it aside.

Squeeze a squiggly line of yellow for the mustard. Let the yellow batter cook, then set it aside.

PLATE

On your dish, lay down the bun first, then the hot dog, and put the mustard on last. Or use regular mustard if that suits your fancy.

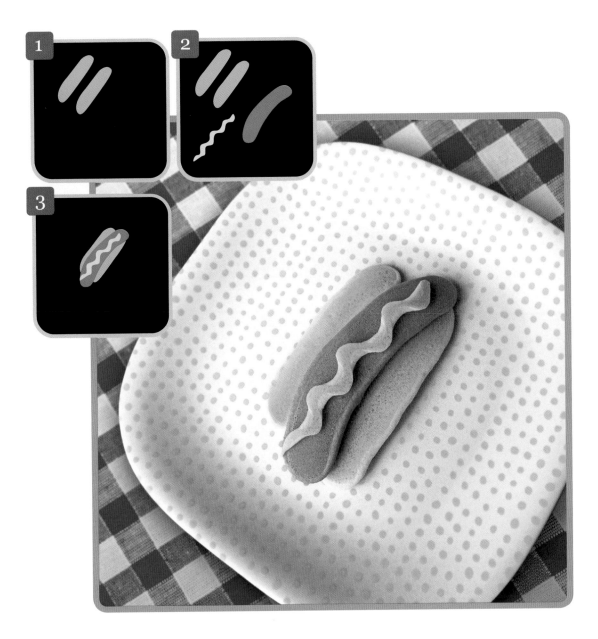

Cherry Pie

. . . .

Pies and pancakes. What a deliciously delightful combination!

PREPARATION

For this recipe, you will need:

- Plain pancake batter
- Natural red food coloring
- Two squeeze bottles (or plastic bags; see page 8)

Split the batter into two parts, one about twice as big as the other, in two separate bowls. Add red food coloring to the smaller portion and keep the larger portion plain. Transfer the batter into two separate squeeze bottles.

CREATE

Let's start with the pie filling. Using your red batter, create a dozen or so small red pancakes. Cook them and set them aside.

Next up, the complex part—the pie crust.

First, make a round pancake to serve as the bottom of the crust. Next, with the plain batter, form a strip of pancake batter big enough to create an enclosed circle when you have it stand, and make it fairly thick. Cook the pieces well, and once they're done, set them up like an actual crust and fill with the red pancake cherries.

Now for the rest of the crust: Lay down six thin strips of batter and cook them with the intent of having some flexibility. You want them somewhat malleable, as you're going to weave them together and place them on top of your pie.

PLATE

Take the crust and create a circle with it. Fill in the crust with the cherry filling and then place the lattice crust on top of the pie. I recommend topping it with whipped cream as part of the whole pie illusion.

Chocolate Chip Cookies

· ·

Chocolate chip cookies? You'll spoil yourself at breakfast.

PREPARATION

For this recipe, you will need:

- Plain pancake batter
- One squeeze bottle (or plastic bag; see page 8)
- Chocolate chips

Transfer the batter into the squeeze bottle.

CREATE

You will want to create as many cookie-size pancakes as you can handle. Cook on one side, then flip, and when they are close to being done, put on some chocolate chips, so they can melt slightly and stick to the pancakes.

PLATE

Arrange the chocolate chip cookie pancakes on a plate to make them look like a plate of cookies. Maybe you can surprise Santa next Christmas with these tricky treats.

7

HOLIDAY THEME PANCAKES

Pierced Heart
(Valentine's Day)

Four-Leaf Clover
(Saint Patrick's
Day)

Easter Chick

American Flag
(Fourth of July)

Ghost and
Pumpkin
(Halloween)

Skull and
Crossbones
(Halloween)

Turkey
(Thanksgiving)

Christmas Tree

Candy Canes
(Christmas)

Pierced Heart (Valentine's Day)

A creation sweet enough for Cupid!

PREPARATION

For this recipe, you will need:

- Plain pancake batter
- Natural red food coloring
- Two squeeze bottles (or plastic bags; see page 8)

Split the batter into two parts in two separate bowls, with one portion twice as big as the other. Add red food coloring to the larger portion and leave the other portion plain. (You may add cocoa powder for a brown arrow.) Transfer the batter into two separate squeeze bottles.

CREATE

The heart is easy enough to create: Just outline a heart pattern on the griddle with the red pancake batter. You want to save a spot in the heart to guide the arrow through; when you fill in the outline with the red batter, leave a small hole in the heart. Flip the pancake, then let it cook thoroughly. Take the heart off the griddle.

Next, draw the arrow. This can be done in one piece and then cut in two to fit through the hole in the heart.

After the arrow is finished cooking, remove it from the griddle.

PLATE

Lay down the heart; half the arrow should be inserted through the hole, and the other half should go under the heart and stick out the back. Add your syrup, and enjoy!

Four-Leaf Clover (Saint Patrick's Day)

It might just be your lucky day after you eat this pancake.

PREPARATION

For this recipe, you will need:

- Plain pancake batter
- Natural green food coloring
- One squeeze bottle (or plastic bag; see page 8)

Color all of the batter with green food coloring, transfer it into a squeeze bottle, and get to pancake-creatin'.

CREATE

This is a really easy pancake. Start with the four-leaf clover outline by making four connecting squarish circle shapes. Fill them all in with the green batter. Off to the side, make a little stem and fill it in.

Once everything is cooked through, remove it from the heat.

PLATE

Place your stem on the plate and add the clover to the top. And top o' the mornin' to ya!

Easter Chick

. . . .

This is a definite Easter surprise for a Sunday! No hunt needed for this egg.

PREPARATION

For this recipe, you will need:

- Plain pancake batter
- Natural green food coloring
- Natural yellow food coloring
- Natural orange food coloring
- Natural red food coloring
- Five squeeze bottles (or plastic bags; see page 8)
- Chocolate chips

Split the batter into five parts in five separate bowls, with about three-fourths divided equally among three bowls, and the remainder divided equally between the remaining two bowls. Add green food coloring to one of the larger portions, yellow to another, and leave the third plain. Add orange food coloring to one of the smaller portions and red to the other.

CREATE

The basket is made in two parts: the container and the handle. First, make the outline of the basket with a few line patterns inside. After cooking the outline, fill in the rest of the basket with the green batter. The handle is cooked the same way—create a basic outline, let it cook for a moment, and fill it in. Set this aside as well.

Now for the egg. Using the plain pancake batter, form a cracked eggshell. Using the orange and red batter, create a pattern inside your eggshell. I went for orange dots and a little swirly red line within the shell. Fill in the rest of the shell with the plain pancake batter, cook, and set it aside.

Now let's make the chick. We need to create only the chick's head, so using the yellow batter, lay down a basic yellow pancake. Using the orange batter, make a small triangle pancake for the beak.

PLATE

Start with the chick's head. Put it on the plate, then place two chocolate chips for eyes and the orange triangle for the beak. Next, place half of the eggshell over a small part at the bottom of the chick's head. Then put the green handles of the basket around the head, almost like a frame. Naturally, the basket comes next. Place the basket on top of the eggshell and the handles. You can place the top half of the eggshell somewhere next to the basket.

American Flag (Fourth of July)

· ·

There's nothing more patriotic than an American flag pancake on the Fourth of July.

PREPARATION

For this recipe, you will need:

- Plain pancake batter
- Natural red food coloring
- Natural blue food coloring
- Three squeeze bottles (or plastic bags; see page 8)

Split the batter into three parts in three separate bowls, with one part half of the batter and the other two parts a quarter of the batter each. Keep the larger portion plain, and add red food coloring to one of the smaller portions and blue food coloring to the other. Transfer the batter into three separate squeeze bottles.

CREATE

First, lay down your outline for the whole flag using plain pancake batter, and for the star section using blue batter, leaving room for the stars and stripes. After cooking the outline thoroughly, start laying down the stripes, in plain and red, like Betsy Ross! For the stars, put down little dots of plain pancake batter within the field where the stars should be. Let them cook before you fill in the rest of the field with the blue pancake batter. Let the flag cook for a few moments, then flip it to cook on the other side.

PLATE

There's not too much to plating this project, though please salute before you eat! Or, if you can, shoot off some fireworks.

Ghost and Pumpkin (Halloween)

Definitely something to think of for Halloween—the ultimate spooky treats.

PREPARATION

For this recipe, you will need:

- Plain pancake batter
- Natural orange food coloring
- Natural green food coloring
- Natural brown food coloring
- Four squeeze bottles (or plastic bags; see page 8)
- Chocolate chips

Split the batter into four parts in four separate bowls, with one portion about a third of the batter and the rest divided into three equal parts. Add orange food coloring to the larger portion of batter, green food coloring to one of the smaller portions, and brown to another. Keep the last portion plain. Transfer the batter into four separate squeeze bottles.

CREATE

The ghost is really easy to make—it's basically a white blob. The trick is to flip it over as soon as possible so that it stays white. You can cook it all the way through on the other side. It's okay if that side browns, as the only side you'll need to show is the lighter side.

For the pumpkin, the trick is to cook the outline and the facial features for as long as possible before you fill in the outline. Add the stem and any flourishes you want.

PLATE

Lay down the pumpkin, and beside it the ghost—before you get slimed! Add chocolate chips for the ghost's eyes, and douse everything in syrup. Just imagine the syrup as the ectoplasmic residue!

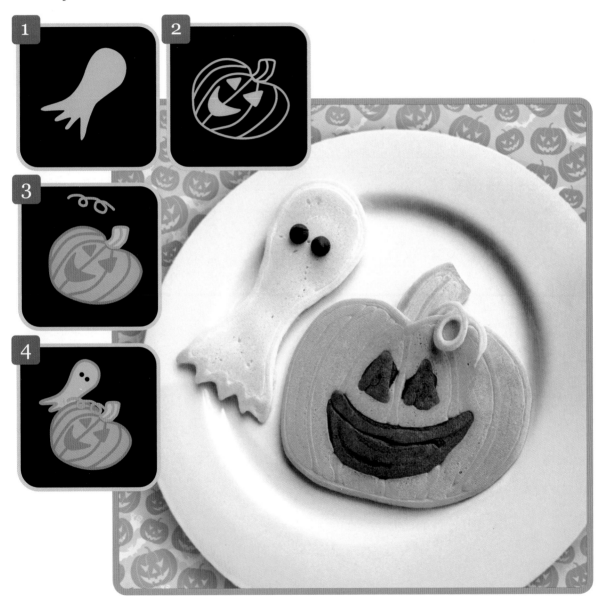

Skull and Crossbones (Halloween)

Arrrrr! Finally, a pancake fit for pirates! This pancake will earn you some "cool mom" or "cool dad" points.

PREPARATION

For this recipe, you will need:

- Plain pancake batter
- One squeeze bottle (or plastic bag; see page 8)

Transfer the batter into a squeeze bottle and you're ready to go!

CREATE

Use the illustration to get an idea for the shape. Get your squeeze bottle in hand and start with the outlines of the skull, eyes, and nostrils. Fill it in, leaving four circles open for the eyes and nose. Finally, make a set of teeth. Flip them all quickly to ensure that one side stays light in color.

Next, draw the outlines of the bones. Fill them in. Try to work quickly, as you don't want to let them brown too much on the griddle.

When the bones are all done cooking, remove them from the heat.

PLATE

Starting with the two crossbones, carefully layer your pancakes as shown. "Yarrrr" now ready to serve. The only danger here is not having enough.

Turkey (Thanksgiving)

This certainly is an unconventional turkey for your Thanksgiving Day celebration. And it definitely requires less prep and cooking time!

PREPARATION

For this recipe, you will need:

- Plain pancake batter
- Natural brown food coloring
- Natural red food coloring
- Three squeeze bottles (or plastic bags; see page 8)

Split the batter into three parts in three separate bowls, with the majority of the batter in one bowl. You need only a tiny amount in the other two bowls. Add brown food coloring to the largest portion and red to one of the other two portions. The last bit is to remain plain. Transfer the batter into three separate squeeze bottles.

CREATE

Make the turkey in three parts: body, tail, and feet. You can choose which one to create first, but I'll start with the body. Using the brown batter, draw the shape of the body, neck, and head. Fill in the outline with the brown batter, leaving a space for the eye. Use some plain batter for the eye, and don't forget the wattle! Use red batter for this.

Next, using the brown pancake batter, form the base of the tail as if you were making a chocolate rainbow. After letting the base cook, draw feather shapes with the red and plain batter and connect them to the base you just cooked. Think of the feathers like the petals of a rose and arrange them that way.

Make the feet by cooking a small shape for them on the griddle. This will be the stand for your finished masterpiece. After you've cooked all the parts of the turkey, assemble the body and tail together like one of those balsa airplanes . . . "Tab A goes into slot B," then put them onto the feet.

PLATE

If you've cooked the turkey properly, plating is going to be easy. Just allow the turkey to stand on the plate, and serve. Carving, of course, is optional. So is the gravy.

Christmas Tree

· ·

It's the most wonderful time of the year . . . pancake time! Just don't peek at the presents too early!

PREPARATION

For this recipe, you will need:

- Plain pancake batter
- Natural green food coloring
- Natural brown food coloring
- Natural yellow food coloring
- Natural red food coloring
- Four squeeze bottles (or plastic bags; see page 8)

Split your pancake batter into four parts in four separate bowls, with about two-thirds in one bowl and the rest equally divided among the other three bowls. Add green food coloring to the larger portion, and the other colors, separately, to each of the other portions. Transfer the batter into four separate squeeze bottles.

CREATE

Let's start with the tree. Using the green batter, make an outline. Make a trunk with brown batter. After letting the tree outline cook for a moment, add some red and yellow dots inside the outline to serve as ornaments. (You can make red bows and yellow ribbons for the presents at this point too, or make them when you make the presents.) Fill in the rest of the tree with the green batter. Let the tree cook thoroughly and set it aside until you are ready to plate it.

Now we'll create the presents. Using the red batter, create an outline of a present along with the bow on top. Make two of these, in fact. Inside each present, use the yellow batter to create the ribbon. Then fill in the rest of the present with the red batter.

PLATE

Place the trunk on the plate first, then put the tree on top. Put the presents at the bottom of the tree, and now you're ready for Christmas morning!

Candy Canes (Christmas)

A winter holiday staple, these little candies just add to the sweetness of breakfast!

PREPARATION

For this recipe, you will need:

- Plain pancake batter
- Natural red food coloring
- Peppermint oil (optional)
- Two squeeze bottles (or plastic bags; see page 8)

Split the batter into two equal parts in two separate bowls. Add red food coloring to one portion and keep the other portion as your plain pancake batter. Add a little peppermint oil to the batter if you like, to make your pancakes more authentic. Transfer the batter into two separate squeeze bottles.

CREATE

Make your candy canes any size you like. Create the outlines first and let them cook for a few minutes, until they have browned just a little. Add the red lines to your candy cane, then fill in the rest with the plain pancake batter.

PLATE

Arrange your candy canes on a plate however you like. I'd also suggest dipping these pancakes in hot cocoa!

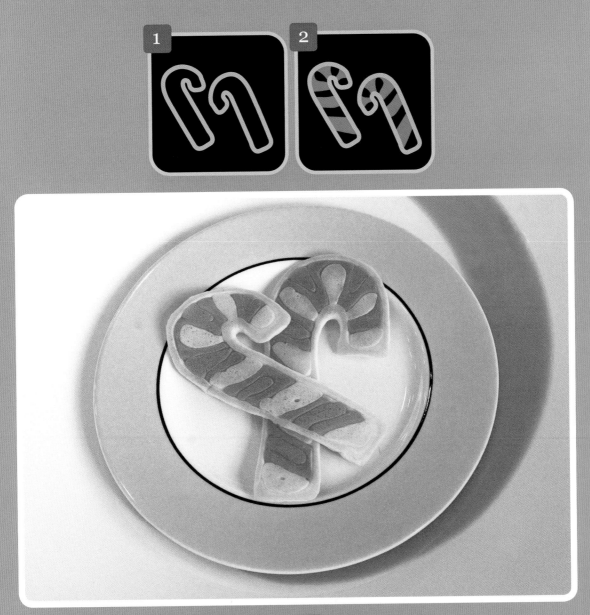
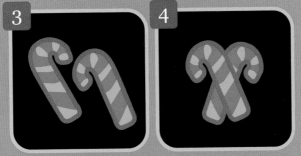

8

ACTIVITIES AND ADVENTURE

Kite

· ·

A pancake made for windy days.

PREPARATION

For this recipe, you will need:

- Plain pancake batter
- Natural red food coloring
- At least one squeeze bottle (or plastic bag; see page 8)

Split the batter into two parts in two separate bowls, one part much larger than the other. You need only a tiny amount for the smaller portion. The small one is to remain plain; add red food coloring to the larger one. Transfer the red batter to a squeeze bottle, and set the plain portion aside. You can add more colors if you choose.

CREATE

With the red batter, make a tall diamond shape. Add a cross to the inside and let it cook just a bit before you fill it in. This will let you see the lines when the kite is fully cooked.

On the side of the griddle, still using your red batter, make a small circle. Next, add the triangles to the sides for the ribbon tie. With your plain batter, make the kite string.

Once everything is cooked through, remove it from the heat.

PLATE

Starting with the string, layer the pieces of the kite on your plate as shown. Hurry and get it to the table before it blows away.

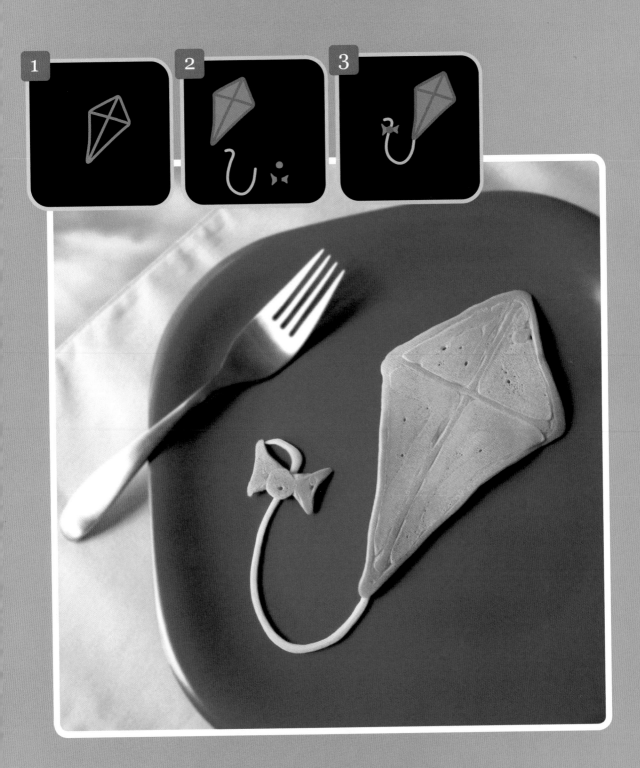

Football

. . . .

Grab your plate and go long. We're bringing the game to breakfast.

PREPARATION

For this recipe, you will need:

- Plain pancake batter
- Natural brown food coloring
- Two squeeze bottles (or plastic bags; see page 8)

Split the batter into two parts in two separate bowls, about three-fourths in one, one-fourth in the other. Add brown food coloring to the larger portion and leave the smaller portion plain. Transfer the batter into two separate squeeze bottles.

CREATE

With your brown batter, make a football shape and fill it in. On the side, using your plain batter, make a line and add small lines to both sides to make the stitches for the football.

When all the pieces are cooked through, remove them from the heat.

PLATE

Lay the football on the plate and place the stitches on top as shown. Game time!

Baseball

Batter up. Breakfast is bound to be a home run today.

PREPARATION

For this recipe, you will need:

- Plain pancake batter
- Natural red food coloring
- One squeeze bottle (or plastic bag; see page 8)

Split your pancake batter into two parts in two separate bowls, the majority in one, a tiny amount in the other. Add red food coloring to the smaller portion and leave the larger portion plain. Transfer the plain batter to a squeeze bottle, and set the red batter aside.

CREATE

With your plain batter, make the outline of a circle. With your red batter, make two half-circles within the large circle for the stitches. You can add little lines to either side as shown. Now fill in the rest with the plain batter.

When the pancake is thoroughly cooked, remove it from the heat.

PLATE

Plate 'em up! Put your pancake on a plate and serve.

Basketball

. . . .

This project is a slam dunk!

PREPARATION

For this recipe, you will need:

- Plain pancake batter
- Natural orange food coloring
- Natural red food coloring
- Natural brown food coloring
- Four squeeze bottles (or plastic bags; see page 8)

Split the batter into four parts in four separate bowls, with about three-fourths of the total in one bowl, and the remainder divided equally among the other three bowls. Add orange food coloring to the large portion; you'll use most of it to fill in the leather of the basketball. Add red food coloring to one of the smaller portions, brown food coloring to the second, and leave the last small portion plain. Transfer the batter into four separate squeeze bottles.

CREATE

Let's start with the basketball. Use the orange batter to create a circle, and use the brown batter to make the grooves of the basketball. Let the outline cook for a moment before adding the rest of the orange batter to fill out the basketball. Set the basketball aside.

Next, we'll create the hoop. Remember to make the hoop large enough so the basketball will fit through it. With the red batter, make an oval for the rim. While letting the red oval cook, use the plain pancake batter to create the net. Start with the basic outline of the net, attaching it to the rim and making sure that the bottom of the net consists of little arcs. Bring down more lines of plain pancake batter to connect to the bottom of the net, then squeeze some diagonal lines across the vertical lines you made. That should give you a rough outline of a basketball net. Let the rim and net cook for a few moments before plating all the elements.

PLATE

Set the basket first: Take the net, which should be connected to the rim, and lay it down on your plate. Now take the basketball and place it inside the hoop. There's nothing like taking this ball to the rack!

Checkers

· ·

Gaming has never been so delicious. Jump your opponent and douse him in syrup! The checker piece, not the person you're actually playing. That would just get sticky.

PREPARATION

For this recipe, you will need:

- Plain pancake batter
- Natural red food coloring
- Natural brown food coloring
- Two squeeze bottles (or plastic bags; see page 8)

Split the batter into two equal parts in two separate bowls. Add red food coloring to one portion and brown food coloring to the other. Transfer the batter into two separate squeeze bottles.

CREATE

For these pancakes, you'll need just two colors. You can opt for different colors, but I like sticking to the traditional red and black (or brown in this case) combination for this one.

Start with the checkerboard. You could try to make an actual checkerboard, but I suggest sticking with a small square, four spaces wide and four spaces for the length. Draw the outline of the board first with the brown pancake batter and let it cook. While it's cooking, take the red batter and start filling in the alternate spaces. Use the brown batter to fill in the rest. Let the board cook for a little longer once you've filled the spaces, flip it over, and cook on the other side.

For the checker pieces, alternate again with the red and brown batter to create small round pancakes.

PLATE

Put the checkerboard on the plate and arrange the pieces however you like. Play a game, capture the pieces, and, naturally, eat them. And then the board!

Tic-Tac-Toe

"A cat's game" here wouldn't be frustrating. It would just create more pancakes to eat. This is a fun pancake to create, especially with the younger ones around. You can play while you cook!

PREPARATION

For this recipe, you will need:

• Plain pancake batter

• One or two squeeze bottles (or plastic bags; see page 8)

Transfer the batter into a squeeze bottle. Have another squeeze bottle handy just in case someone would like to play you!

CREATE

For this game, you need just the plain pancake batter, but you can opt for different colors as well.

Start with the board, drawing out two horizontal lines that intersect two vertical lines. After that, go ahead and play the game with some of the remaining batter. X's go first!

PLATE

Once the game is done and the pancakes have been cooked, transfer them to the plate. If you actually had a cat's game, you could keep playing with your food before eating it.

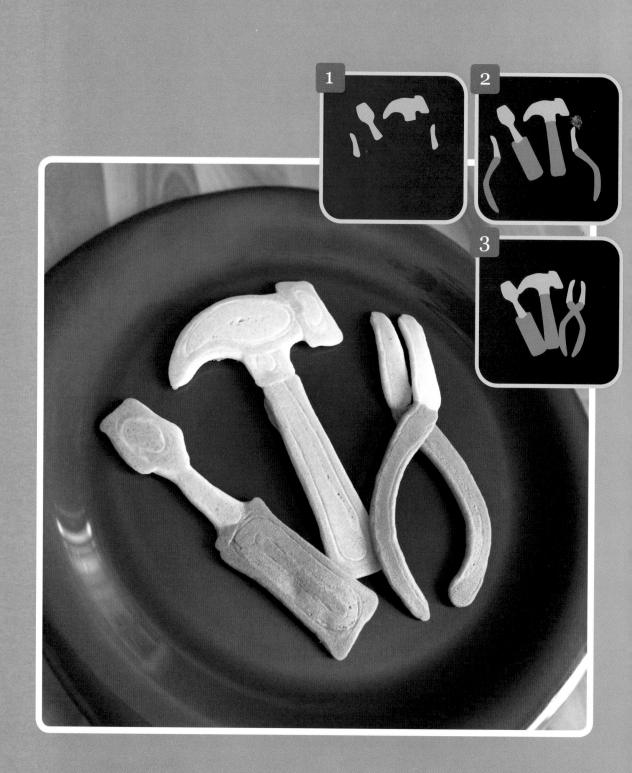

Tools

These are the only tools you'll need to fix up a great breakfast. A DIY project that'll get everyone excited for the morning.

PREPARATION

For this recipe, you will need:
- Plain pancake batter
- Natural red food coloring
- Natural orange food coloring
- Three squeeze bottles (or plastic bags; see page 8)

Split the batter into three equal parts in three separate bowls. Add red food coloring to one of the portions and orange to another. Leave the last portion plain. Transfer the batter into three separate squeeze bottles.

CREATE

Naturally, you can choose to create any tool you'd like, but for this one, we'll start with three basics: hammer, screwdriver, and pliers.

Let's start with the hammer. First put down an outline for the hammer's head using the plain pancake batter. After letting the hammer outline cook, fill in the rest of the hammer and start with the handle. Make the outline using the orange batter, connecting it to the hammer's head as you make it. Fill in the rest of the handle with the orange batter.

The screwdriver follows the essential blueprint of the hammer, except the handles will be made with the red batter. Make an outline for the head of the screwdriver with the plain batter and lay down the red batter for the handle, making sure that the wet batter is connected to the rest of the screwdriver. Let it cook for a few moments before flipping it.

With the pliers, you'll need to be quick. Lay down the outline of one of the grips with the red pancake batter and immediately take the squeeze bottle with the plain pancake batter to lay out the head of the tool and fill it in. Repeat with the other side of the pliers. Don't attach the pieces until you plate the pancake.

PLATE

The hammer and the screwdriver are easy—just place them on your plate. The pliers are easy too—just lay them down, one on top of the other, to make it look like the levers are attached at a pivot. You can serve all the tools with syrup instead of WD-40.

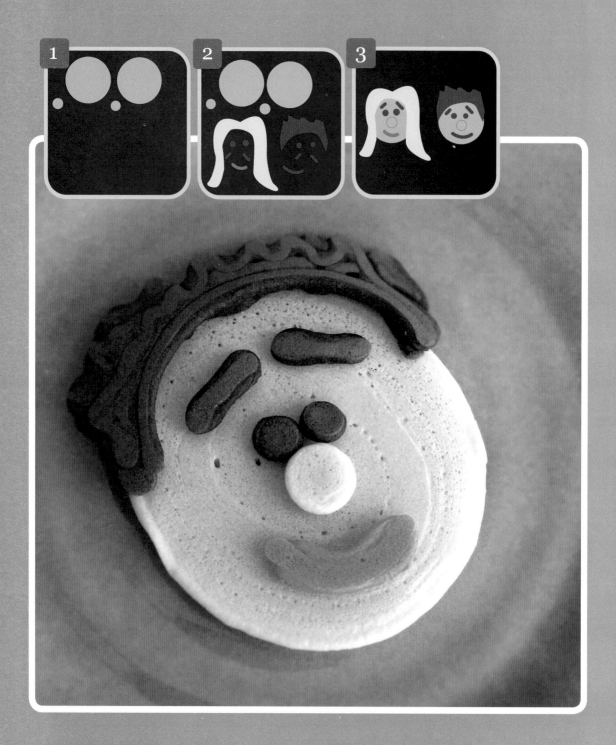

Portrait

. . . .

"A portrait is a mirror to the soul."

Okay, I just made up that quotation. Anyway, this simple portrait pancake can be adjusted however you like, depending on the subject of your pancake. I'll give you the basics so you can create like a Pancake Picasso!

PREPARATION

For this recipe, you will need:
- Plain pancake batter
- Natural brown food coloring
- Natural red food coloring
- Natural yellow food coloring
- Four squeeze bottles (or plastic bags; see page 8)

Split the batter into four parts in four separate bowls, two smaller portions and two larger; the larger portions should be about twice as large as the smaller. Add brown food coloring to one of the smaller portions and red food coloring to the other smaller portion. Add yellow food coloring to one of the larger portions and keep the other large portion as plain batter. Transfer the batter into four separate squeeze bottles.

CREATE

Using the plain batter, cook a regular round pancake and set it aside. Depending on your choice of hair color (and gender), squeeze out the basic outline of the hair you'd like your portrait to have. You can even create a mohawk if you like. That's the creative license you have! Fill in the rest of the outline of the hair, cook it for a few moments, and set it aside.

Next, we'll work on the separate features of the face—the eyes, eyebrows, nose, and mouth. With the brown batter, lay out two very thin lines for the eyebrows. Watch as they cook, so you can remove them from the heat when you must. Form the lips with the red batter (or even the brown), and set a smile or a frown, depending on your mood. Use the brown batter to make two small dots for the eyes.

The last step is to create a small pancake using the plain batter. This will serve as the nose. Cook it carefully and remove all parts from the griddle.

PLATE

Layer the piece, starting with the round pancake for the head and setting the hair on top of it. Next, put down the eyes and eyebrows, the nose, and the mouth. Voilà! A portrait worthy of a Pancake Picasso!

Guitar

· ·

Practice at breakfast!

PREPARATION

For this recipe, you will need:

- Plain pancake batter
- Natural red food coloring
- Natural brown food coloring
- Three squeeze bottles (or plastic bags; see page 8)

Split your pancake batter into three parts in three separate bowls, one larger portion about three-fourths of the total, and the rest divided into two equal portions. Add red food coloring to the larger portion and brown food coloring to one of the smaller portions. Leave the last portion plain. Transfer the batter into three separate squeeze bottles.

CREATE

First, draw your guitar outline with the red batter and then fill it, leaving a hole as illustrated. With the brown batter, make a rather thick brown line to fit into the top of the guitar body; add little brown dots at the top for the tuning pegs. Fill the hole in the guitar with brown batter. Cook the pancake and then flip it over gently. When it is fully cooked, set it aside.

With the plain batter, make the frets—several separate short horizontal lines—and the strings—three long, thin lines. Cook them until they are stiff and then carefully remove them from the heat.

PLATE

Take your guitar and place it on the plate. Carefully position the frets and strings. Shred
that baby while you snack away.

Rocket Ship

· ·

What better way to launch the day than a rocket ship for breakfast.

PREPARATION

For this recipe, you will need:

- Plain pancake batter
- Natural red food coloring
- Natural green food coloring
- Natural yellow food coloring
- Four squeeze bottles (or plastic bags; see page 8)

Split the batter into four parts in four separate bowls, with half of the batter in one bowl and the other half divided equally among the other three bowls. Keep the larger portion plain. Add red food coloring to one of the smaller portions, green to another, and yellow to the third. Transfer the batter into four separate squeeze bottles and you're ready to go!

CREATE

Let's begin with the rocket body. Make an elongated teardrop outline with your plain batter. Fill it in, leaving an open circle up toward the top.

Now, with your red batter, make two fins at the bottom of the rocket body. Attach them to the actual body so you don't have to layer later. Make the flames with your yellow batter and attach them to the bottom of your ship.

Off to the side of the griddle, make a green circle for the planet. With your plain batter, make an oval, but don't fill it in. This will serve as Saturn's Ring.

When all the pieces are finished cooking, remove them from the heat.

PLATE

Place the rocket on the plate. Take the planet and slide it into Saturn's Ring.

3-2-1 . . . breakfast time!

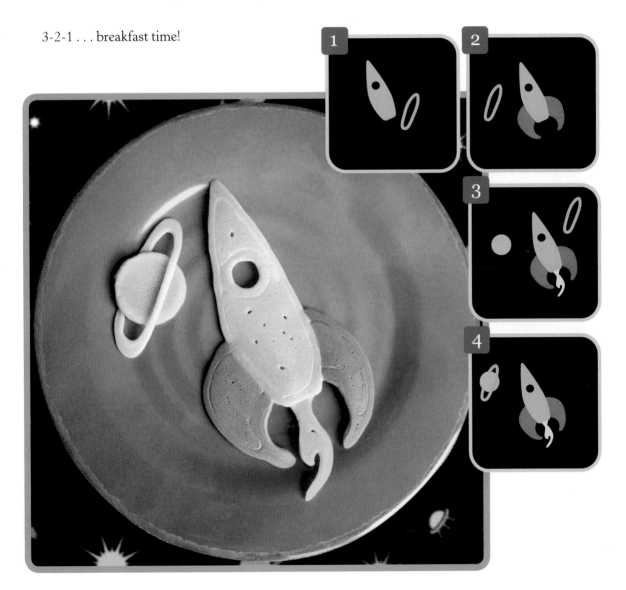

Bomb

. . . .

You dropped the bomb on . . . my plate! Good thing real bombs aren't this easy to make.

PREPARATION

For this recipe, you will need:

- Plain pancake batter
- Natural brown food coloring
- Natural red food coloring
- Three squeeze bottles (or plastic bags; see page 8)

Split the batter into three parts in three separate bowls, one with about three-fourths of the batter, and the rest of the batter divided equally between the other two bowls. Add brown food coloring to the larger portion. Add red food coloring to one of the smaller portions and leave the other one plain. Transfer the batter into three separate squeeze bottles. You can add more colors if you choose.

CREATE

Let's grab our brown batter and start by making an outline of a large circle and filling it in. Attach a small rectangle to one side of the bomb.

Take your plain batter and make a little line off to the side for the bomb string. Make four or five small lines with the red batter for the sparks.

Once everything is cooked through, remove it from the heat.

PLATE

Place your bomb on the plate. Take your fuse string and slide the tip of one side just under the rectangle on the bomb. Now add the sparks. This pancake is exploding in flavor!

Submarine

We all live . . . in a pancake submarine! Submerge yourself in a creation that Captain Nemo would be proud of!

PREPARATION

For this recipe, you will need:

- Plain pancake batter
- Natural blue food coloring
- Two squeeze bottles (or plastic bags; see page 8)

Split the batter into two parts in two separate bowls, one with about three-fourths of the batter and the other with the remainder. Add blue food coloring to the smaller portion and leave the larger portion plain. Transfer the batter into two separate squeeze bottles.

CREATE

Start with the outline of the submarine using the plain batter and immediately lay down three small round blue pancakes within the frame of the submarine. Let them cook for a few moments, then fill in the rest of the submarine's frame with the plain batter. Flip the submarine over, let it cook on the other side, and you're ready for the dry dock!

PLATE

Take the submarine from the griddle, submerge it in syrup, and enjoy. If you like, you can also make an octopus pancake (see page 42) to create the pancake equivalent of a literary classic!

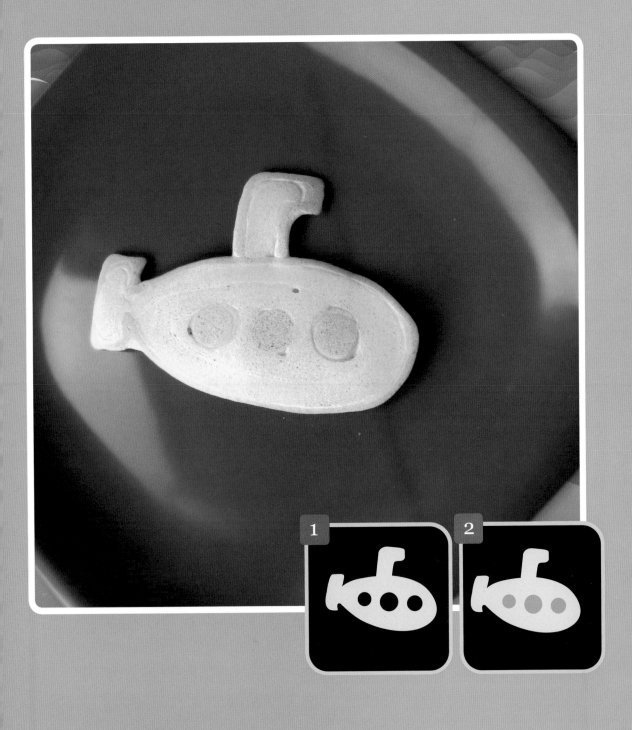

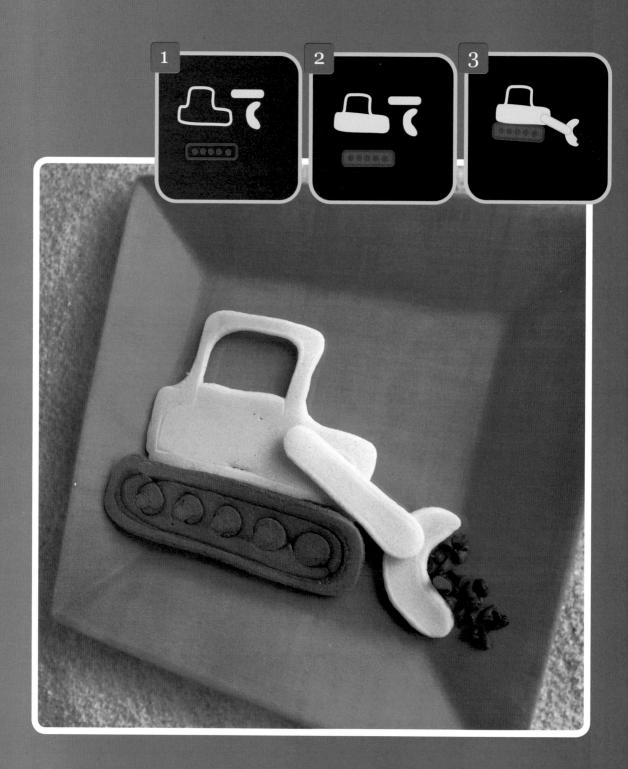

Bulldozer

I've found this one is a hit with most boys!

PREPARATION

For this recipe, you will need:

- Plain pancake batter
- Natural brown food coloring
- Two squeeze bottles (or plastic bags; see page 8)
- Chocolate chips

Split the pancake batter into two equal parts in two separate bowls. Add brown food coloring to one portion and leave the other plain. Make sure your brown batter is rather dark. Transfer the batter into two separate squeeze bottles.

CREATE

Starting with the brown batter, let's create the bulldozer tracks: Lay down an outline of the tracks as a rounded rectangle. Then place four or five small circles inside as the wheels. Fill in the rest of the tracks and let this cook for a few moments. After letting this brown a little, set the tracks aside for plating.

Now for the rest of the bulldozer. You'll need to create three basic parts: the bulldozer housing and canopy, the blade, and its arm. First, with the plain batter, make a basic rectangular pancake, a little shorter than the length of the bulldozer tracks, and a square outline on top of the rectangle for the driver. Yes, you could create a driver as well, though it's entirely up to you.

Now to create the blade and the arm. First, lay down a crescent moon using the plain pancake batter. Let that cook for a few moments, and then lay down a strip of plain pancake batter to use as the arm. As with the blade, let this cook for a little before plating.

PLATE

Place the bulldozer housing and canopy pancake on the plate first. Put the bulldozer tracks second, laying it slightly over the bottom of the bulldozer. Next, place the arm and the blade on the bulldozer, making it look as if the arm and blade are attached. Last, place a few chocolate chips in front of or near the blade, to create the illusion that the bulldozer is moving dirt.

Wand

· ·

From Harry Potter to Gandalf, every wizard would appreciate this pancake. This will make an appetite "magically" disappear!

PREPARATION

For this recipe, you will need:

- Plain pancake batter
- Natural red food coloring
- Natural yellow food coloring
- Three squeeze bottles (or plastic bags; see page 8)

Split your pancake batter into three equal parts in three separate bowls. Add red food coloring to one portion and yellow to another; leave the last plain. Transfer the batter into three separate squeeze bottles.

CREATE

This is a relatively simple pancake. We'll start with the star: Using the red batter or pink batter, depending on the degree of the coloring you used, lay down a thick outline of a star on your griddle. After finishing the outline of the star, put a small diamond (or circle) in the middle of the star with the red batter.

Fill in the area between the two red sections of the star with the yellow batter. Let the pancake star cook for a few moments before creating the wand handle separately.

Depending on your taste, you could also use brown batter for the handle or just stick with the plain pancake batter. Either way, the wand handle is just a simple pancake strip, so lay one down on your griddle and cook it accordingly. Now you're ready to plate!

PLATE

Set down the wand handle first. Then take the star for the top of your wand and lay it down on the handle. Conjure up some syrup and butter and you're ready to eat. Merlin would be proud of you!

Mount Pancake

· ·

This creation is as easy as climbing a mountain. . . . Okay, maybe that's not the greatest comparison.

PREPARATION

For this recipe, you will need:

- Plain pancake batter
- One squeeze bottle (or plastic bag; see page 8)

Transfer the batter into a squeeze bottle and you're ready to go!

CREATE

Create a few plain round pancakes, making them increasingly smaller in size. Create a few pancake O's to top off the volcano.

PLATE

Stack one pancake on top of the other, from largest to smallest, saving the pancake O's for the top. Pour some syrup down the side of the volcano and let some drop into the top of the volcano. Just watch for syrup eruptions!

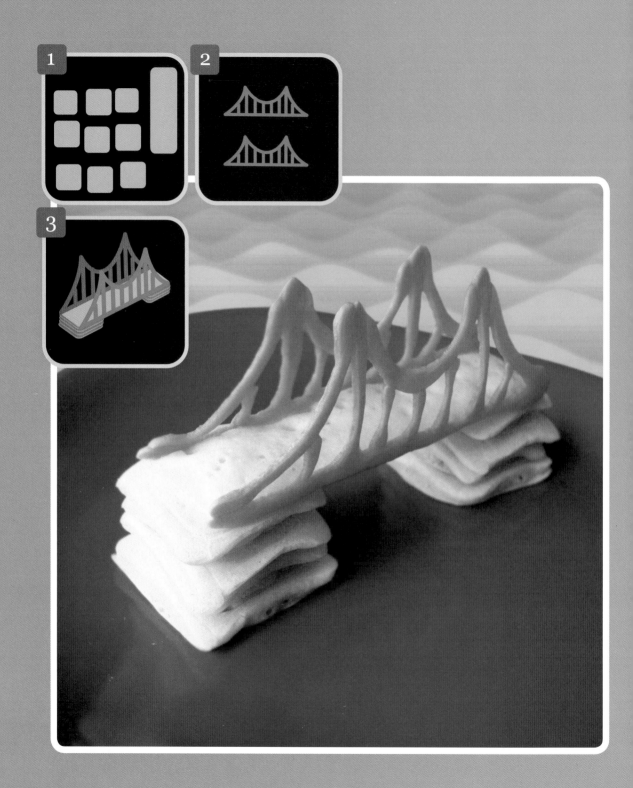

Golden Gate Bridge

. . . .

No toll needed for this, just patience and an ability to withstand some heat from the griddle!

PREPARATION

For this recipe, you will need:

- Plain pancake batter
- Natural red food coloring
- Two squeeze bottles (or plastic bags; see page 8)

Split the batter into two parts, with one part three-fourths of the batter. Add red food coloring to the smaller portion, and keep the other plain. Transfer the batter into two separate squeeze bottles.

CREATE

First, lay down several squares of plain pancake batter for the piers. If you overcook these pieces, that's okay. That way they will become pretty stable, almost like balsa wood. The trick is to cook out all the moisture without burning the pancakes. Now make the supports for the bridge using the red pancake batter; cook them well.

Next, draw the road deck with plain batter; it's basically a rectangle. As it's cooking, place the red supports into the batter and stand them up vertically. After assembling the supports to the road deck, leave your bridge on the griddle for a few minutes to solidify everything. You might have to hold the pieces in place with your fingers until the road deck finishes cooking.

PLATE

Stack your square pancakes one atop another in two piles, adding some height for the bridge. Then place the bridge on the piers, and there you have it. For even more fun and maybe some revenue, you could try building a tollbooth too.

You could also cook a meandering strip of pancake with blue batter to look like a body of water, and book-end the water with some plain-batter or brown-batter shore. Cook additional rectangular plain or brown pancakes to serve as hills.

9

JUST FOR FUN

Balloons

· ·

Here's another way to brighten up breakfast! These balloons won't fly away in a gentle breeze.

PREPARATION

For this recipe, you will need:

- Plain pancake batter
- Natural red food coloring
- Natural yellow food coloring
- Natural green food coloring
- Four squeeze bottles (or plastic bags; see page 8)

Split the batter into four parts in four separate bowls; three of them will be equal in size and the fourth will have just a tiny amount of batter for the balloon strings. Add one food coloring to each of the three large portions of batter. Save the last, small portion as the plain pancake batter. Transfer the batter into four separate squeeze bottles.

CREATE

The best way to create the shape of the balloons is to think of them as lightbulbs with a thinner base. Using the red, yellow, and green batters, outline your balloons and then fill them in. You could use other colors as well, but we'll stick with these for now.

As you're cooking the balloons, use the plain batter to create the strings for your balloons. Attach them at the base of your balloons. Let them cook, then set them aside.

PLATE

Be careful that these balloons don't fly away (don't you hate it when they're just out of reach?), and lay them down on your plate. Serve with syrup and enjoy!

Smiley Face

This dish definitely will put a smile on your face!

PREPARATION

For this recipe, you will need:

- Plain pancake batter
- Natural brown food coloring
- Natural yellow food coloring
- Two squeeze bottles (or plastic bags; see page 8)

Split the batter into two parts in two separate bowls, one with about three-fourths of the batter and the other with the remainder. Add brown food coloring to the small amount and add yellow food coloring to the rest. Transfer the batter into two separate squeeze bottles.

CREATE

Taking the squeeze bottle with the yellow batter, lay down a normal round pancake and let it cook. While it's cooking, take the squeeze bottle with brown batter and create the eyes and the smile off to the side. Let all the pieces brown a little, flip them, and finish cooking.

PLATE

Nothing complicated about this one. Just set the yellow pancake down first and then the eyes and mouth on top. This is guaranteed to turn any frown upside down!

Earrings and Bracelet

· ·

There isn't much to the creation of this latest fashion craze, but its street value is undeniable!

PREPARATION

For this recipe, you will need:

- Plain pancake batter
- One squeeze bottle (or plastic bag; see page 8)

Transfer the batter into a squeeze bottle and you're ready to go!

CREATE

Lay down a few pancake rings on your griddle, making sure they're big enough for the hands and wrists of those you're "fashioning" them for. Let the accessories cook thoroughly before letting the kids dress up!

Think twice about applying syrup. The fashion police might end up tagging you!

PLATE

Plating is optional for this recipe. You can wear them out, though you should take them off before eating.

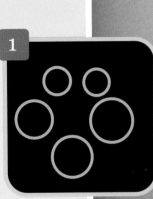

Sunglasses

· ·

The future's so bright you've got to wear . . . well, eat pancake shades!

For this recipe, you will need:
- Plain pancake batter
- One squeeze bottle (or plastic bag; see page 8)

Transfer the batter into a squeeze bottle and you're ready to go!

CREATE

This one is easy enough to create: Make an outline of two circle pancakes and arms, attaching the arms to the circles as shown. Then connect the circles with a little bridge to complete the glasses.

PLATE

You can certainly plate this piece, though really you should wear it!

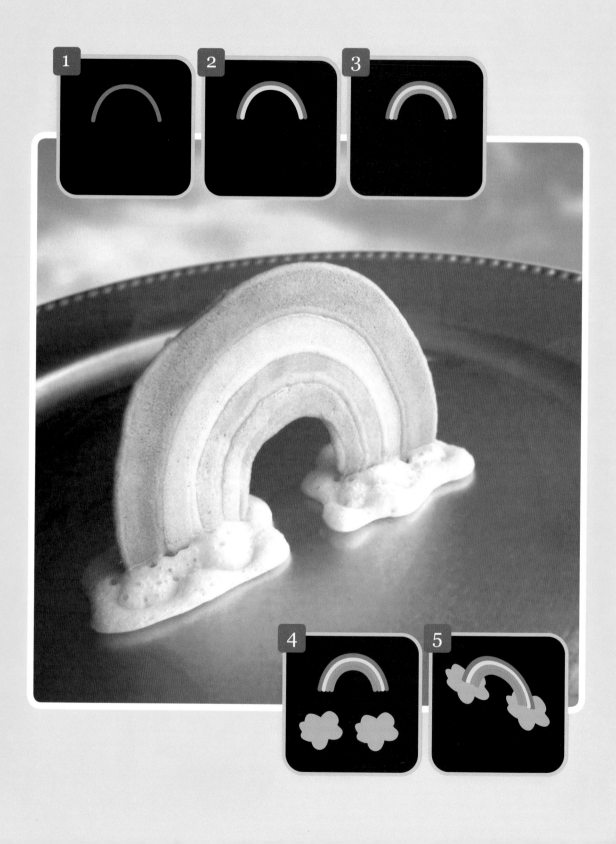

Rainbow

· ·

Somewhere over this rainbow is . . . just a pot of syrup, which could be worth
something to someone!

PREPARATION

For this recipe, you will need:

- Plain pancake batter
- Natural red food coloring
- Natural blue food coloring
- Natural yellow food coloring
- Natural green food coloring
- Five squeeze bottles (or plastic bags; see page 8)

Split the batter into five equal parts in five separate bowls. Add one color to each of four
portions, and leave one portion plain. Transfer the batter into five separate squeeze
bottles.

CREATE

Start with the rainbow by using the colors in your squeeze bottles for each of the layers.
You can arrange them however you want, though if you'd like to get technical, start with
the red on the outside, then use the yellow and the green, and end with the blue inside.
Cook thoroughly on both sides and set it aside.

Using the plain batter, form the clouds: Start with the outlines of two clouds and let them
cook for a moment.

Here's where it gets tricky, for a 3-D version. Take the completed rainbow and set the ends inside the two cloud outlines. With the squeeze bottle of plain batter, fill in the rest of each cloud, and let each one cook into a leg of the rainbow. After a moment, test the rainbow's stability—see if it can stand on its own. If not, you can simply lay it down and make it look like the rainbow is coming out of the clouds.

PLATE

If you were going for the 3-D rainbow, hopefully it will stand on its own. Move it to the plate to enjoy. Or lay it down and enjoy it anyway. Just check for any leprechauns lurking nearby!

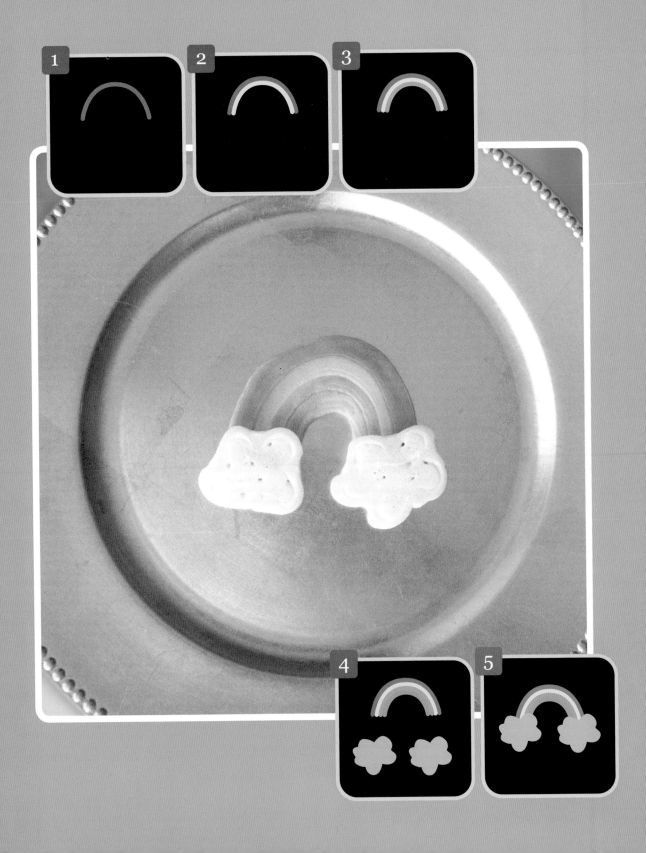

Bling

· ·

This is a creation to wear with style!

PREPARATION

For this recipe, you will need:

- Plain pancake batter
- One squeeze bottle (or plastic bag; see page 8)

Transfer the batter into a squeeze bottle and you're ready to go!

CREATE

This one isn't too complex, but it's fairly time-consuming. First, create as many C pancakes as you need for the length of the chain. Next, link them together.

Finally, make a cool medallion to hang from your bling.

PLATE

Just wear it and bling it. Add swagger if you need to!

Flower Pot

· ·

Dads, score some points with Mom with this recipe. Or brighten any little girl's day.

PREPARATION

For this recipe, you will need:

- Plain pancake batter
- Natural red food coloring
- Natural green food coloring
- Natural yellow food coloring
- Natural brown food coloring
- Five squeeze bottles (or plastic bags; see page 8)
- Sprinkles (optional)

Split the batter equally among five bowls, and prepare plain, red, green, yellow, and brown portions. Transfer the batter into five separate squeeze bottles.

CREATE

Let's start easy and make the pot. Outline with the brown batter and then fill it in. When it is cooked, set it aside.

Time for the flowers. Using the plain batter, start with the center of the flower as a circle. Then draw the outline of the petals. Fill in the petals of each flower with the yellow batter and red batter.

For the stems and leaves, get your green batter ready. Make the stems of varying lengths and add some leaves.

Once they are cooked, remove all the pieces from the heat.

PLATE

Make your flower arrangement, layering the flower heads and stems on the plate. Place the pot over the bottoms of the stems. To make the flowers really sparkle, add some fun sprinkles. *Bon appétit!*

Artist's Palette

This is a masterpiece waiting to happen. Stir your kids' creative juices with this pancake.

PREPARATION

For this recipe, you will need:

- Plain pancake batter
- Natural brown food coloring
- Natural green food coloring
- Natural red food coloring
- Natural yellow food coloring
- Natural blue food coloring
- Six squeeze bottles (or plastic bags; see page 8)

Split the batter into six equal parts in six separate bowls. Add one color to each of five portions, and leave one portion plain. Transfer the batter into six separate squeeze bottles.

CREATE

Which came first, the palette or the paint? In our case, we'll start with the palette. Grab your plain-batter squeeze bottle and begin making the outline of the palette. Fill it in, leaving one open hole near the top. On the side, make the paintbrush stick outline and fill it in.

Now we need some paint and brush bristles. With the brown batter, make the bristles of the brush, attaching them to the stick. Then make one small swirly circle with each color.

When they are all done cooking, remove them from the heat.

PLATE

Lay your palette on the plate first. Now you can add the paint and paintbrush. Voilà! It's time to paint some syrup on.

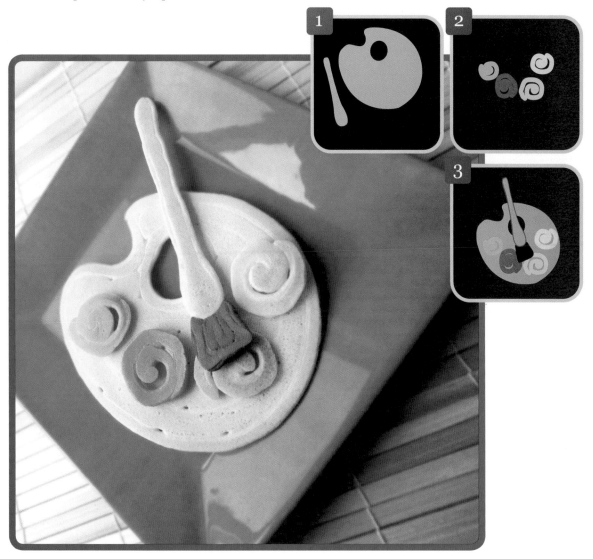

Alien

. . . .

It's a Pancake Encounter of the Third Kind! This fun creation is truly out of this world.

PREPARATION

For this recipe, you will need:

- Plain pancake batter
- Natural green food coloring
- Natural brown food coloring
- Three squeeze bottles (or plastic bags; see page 8)
- Chocolate chips

Split your pancake batter into three parts in three separate bowls: two larger portions, each a little more than a third of the batter, and one smaller portion. Add green food coloring to one of the larger portions, and leave the other larger portion plain. Add brown food coloring to the smaller portion. (You may want to alter the colors and preportions; see the variations illustrated.)

CREATE

Let's start with the flying saucer. Create an oval outline for the saucer with the plain batter or the green, and let it cook for a few moments. Inside the oval, lay down a line of green or brown dots for the windows. Fill in the rest of the saucer with plain or green pancake batter, and make a dome for the saucer (or this can be the alien's arms), as illustrated, with the green batter. Cook the saucer and dome and set aside.

There are several ways to create the alien, but we'll use a basic shape—similar to a lightbulb—for this one. Make the outline with the green batter and let it cook for a moment, then fill in the rest of the alien and cook. Our last step will be the smile for the alien, for which we'll use the brown batter. Just a simple little crescent will do.

PLATE

Place the saucer with its dome on the plate. Insert the alien, then add his smile, and two chocolate chips for his eyes. Now it's warp speed to delicious!

Fishbowl

· ·

Fish are supposed to be soothing for your nerves. This fishbowl soothes your appetite!

PREPARATION

For this recipe, you will need:

- Plain pancake batter
- Natural orange food coloring (optional)
- One or two squeeze bottles (or plastic bags; see page 8)

Transfer the batter into a squeeze bottle and you're ready to go!

CREATE

Start by making an outline for the fishbowl. At the bottom, you'll want to create a layer of pebbles as well. You may want to vary the colors—use orange batter for the pebbles (and next, the fish) if you like. After letting the outline cook a little, fill in the rest of the bottom of the fishbowl with plain batter.

Create a few fish to put inside the fishbowl. Now it's time to plate!

PLATE

Plating is easy enough. Just lay down the fishbowl and place the fish inside the bowl. Now you're ready to relax . . . and eat!

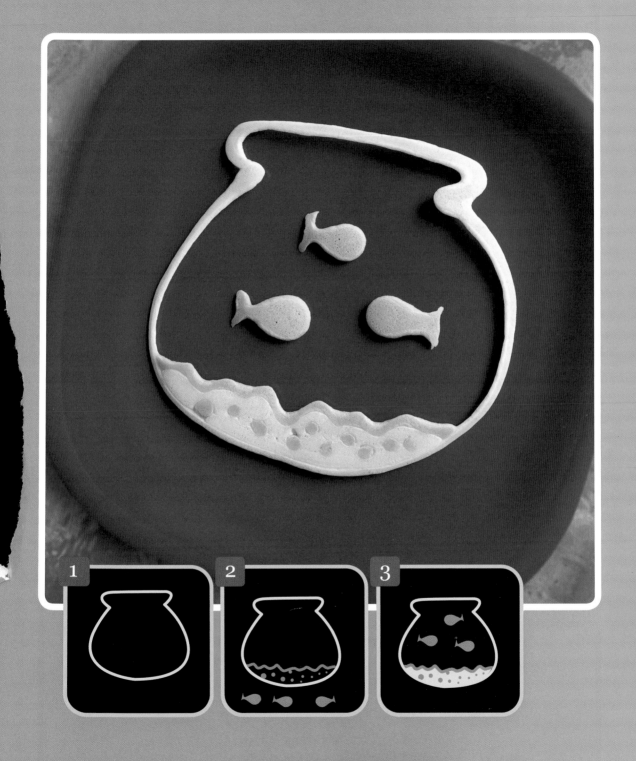